NAU!

MISSION INSPIRED

*With Best Wishes
&
Inspirational Reading!*

John P. Nau

1979

NAU!

MISSION INSPIRED

by

John F. Nau

CLAYTON PUBLISHING HOUSE, INC.

St. Louis, Mo. 63117

Nau! Mission Inspired

John F. Nau

PREFACE

Hebrews 13:7 is basis enough for recalling in writing and copying in word and deed the life and works of teachers of the Word, such as Dr. Henry Nau, who has run his course and is now sleeping with the fathers, his works following him.

Dr. Nau's son, John F. Nau, one of seven children, herewith records the life of this God-made "missionary, philologist, educator, theologian, father, friend, and above all, humanitarian."

Like many other biographies of faithful religious leaders, this one presents throughout, like a thread through a garment, the manifestation of God's glory, man's insufficiency, and God's grace in calling and equipping His servants for His cause — the salvation of souls.

Yet, this biography is *sui generis,* in a class to itself. Largely, it is an eye witness, chronological, living account portraying details, as from a diary, and furnishing first-hand information on missions in India, Africa, and elsewhere, which otherwise would have been lost forever. Also it sets forth more than two decades of a high school and college president's ups and downs in a unique institution. And outstanding is its documentation of a missionary's zeal to re-enter the mission field, of his delight in the waning years of his life, and the actual performance of his duties in that field.

Actors have said that they make fiction look like truth, whereas some ministers make truth look like fiction. Not so, John Nau. His is a presentation of the truth, plainly and elegantly told. "How forcible are right words!" And this in itself is a miracle of God's grace. A foreign lad comes to America, knowing absolutely nothing of the language, and under parental guidance and exposure to salutary influences of education rises to a brilliant command of the language and a professorship of philosophy at the University of Southern Mississippi.

In this life story we see how the Lord of the Church again and again uses His unsearchable ways and judgments to work things out for the coming of His ruling power of grace in the hearts of men. Because of this Dr. Nau became a missionary par excellence, a linguist of the first order, who mastered more languages than one can count on the fingers of both hands, one round. He learned and practiced the art of distinguishing well and teaching well. Whenever our Lord's mission directive "Go" came to him, he went with unflagging, tireless heart, hand, and voice. This is how John truthfully pictures him in this biography.

Here and there we find some Teutonic brashness, bordering on inexpediency. From my own experience with Dr. Nau I could add a few examples bearing this out, as when he would say to a pupil: "Here is the Isle of Rhodes! Here dance!" Or: "Don't stand there looking at me like a cow!" Or how he was engaged in fisticuffs with a student who was the champ boxer on the campus at Luther College. The chap had to run, with "Doc" in hot pursuit. Such traits and weaknesses Dr. Nau often acknowledged.

This Germanic, laconic, terse, curt characteristic, not ordinarily conducive to close relationship with Negroes, was not an insurmountable wall with Dr.

Nau, who related superbly with Blacks. His loving concern was the leavening influence.

Eternity alone will reveal the extent of his influence upon myriads of souls. Like the riplet, it reached the undersigned fifty years ago, getting him to Immanuel Lutheran College, Greensboro, North Carolina, to study three years for the ministry, after four years under his tutelage at Luther College in New Orleans. Dr. Nau secured financial help by putting an appeal in the *Missionstaube*, stating that it was for a boy who showed promise. A Mr. Ernest from Thiensville, Wisconsin, responded and paid two years of the schooling.

"Whose faith follow." — This biography will have served its purpose if we remember Dr. H. Nau and follow in his footsteps.

As he did: Forget the sins and shame of the past, buried in the wounds of Christ.

Spend and be spent for Christ, to gain some.

Make the most of God-given talents.

Be a Good Samaritan to the downtrodden and the lowly especially, and to all who need our love.

Let the spiritual have priority over the earthly.

Contend for the faith.

Be proud of the Church of the Reformation.

Die in the Lord!

A. Dominick

Mobile, Alabama

ACKNOWLEDGMENTS

With gratitude I recognize the assistance given me by the presidents of the University of Southern Mississippi, Dr. W.D. McCain and Dr. Aubrey K. Lucas. Their generous financial support made it possible to gather the material necessary to write this biography and to receive the much-needed secretarial work, without which the completion of this effort would have been nearly impossible.

To the members of my immediate family, particularly my wife, Johanna, my son, Henry, and my sister, Mary Ann, who, by their constant encouragement and willing assistance in gathering vital research materials, enlivened my spirit to continue a task which occupied a great deal of my energy and time during the past twenty years; to the curator, Dr. August Suelflow, of the Concordia Historical Archives of St. Louis, Missouri, and his competent staff, whose interest in gathering, preserving, and classifying innumerable letters, articles, and other data, which shed light on the life and labors of Henry Nau, have lightened the historian's task; to the many individuals who knew and worked with missionary Nau and who were more than willing to share their knowledge of experiences with him — to all these I am most deeply indebted. To my scholarly and competent coworker and friend, Dr. Lynnwood Orange, for the painstaking effort of reading the manuscript and offering invaluable counsel, I express my personal appreciation. To Mrs. Barbara Carlisle Poole, who not only helped prepare copy for publication but through her joyful spirit and personal interest, made the otherwise drab part of this task a joy and a pleasure, I express my thanks. Apparent infelicities in the reproduction of Henry Nau's conversation and correspondence are not to be charged to her account but to the workings of Henry's agitated Teutonic mind that often ignored some of the more pedestrian rules of grammar. Occasionally I have introduced some clarification.

Although I gladly take the responsibility for everything and anything that has been written in this biography, I know that I owe to many, many others appreciation and thanks. To everyone who had any part, large or small, in bringing about the fulfillment of a dream that I had shortly after the death of Henry Nau, my father, I say, "Thank you!" I hope that their efforts, together with mine, will bring many meaningful moments to everyone who will read the life and mission of Henry Nau, Mission Inspired.

John F. Nau
Hattiesburg, Mississippi

CHAPTER 1

On an October night in 1902 a dejected figure walked haltingly in the lower area of Manhattan, New York. Loneliness engulfed him as he pressed his way through the darkness. He had come to New York to make it big, but in a short time he lost everything he owned, except a small monetary gift his mother had pressed into his hands before he began his wanderings. Now, at 21 years of age, he decided to end his life.

As he made his way to the murky and treacherous waters of the East River, he glanced at a sign, *Pilger Haus*. One upward look changed his direction. The man whom the future would identify as missionary, philologist, educator, theologian, father, friend, and humanitarian entered the Home for Travelers.

On his entry into the *Pilger Haus,* he introduced himself to two Lutheran pastors, Stephanus Keyl and Otto H. Restin. "I am Henry Nau." Accustomed to delinquent young men, Keyl and Restin engaged Henry in a rather lengthy conversation. They wanted to learn as much as possible about him, for he was articulate, bright, and, although depressed at the time, showed a hidden store of vitality. Keyl noticed an ugly mark on his forehead and asked: "How did you manage to receive such a scar?"

For the first time in his life Henry felt ashamed of the scar, which until that moment had been a mark of pride and heroism. With some hesitation he answered, "The scar is the result of a duel — a duel fought without the consent of my father."

"What happened then?" asked Keyl.

The question opened a series of confessions.

"In the fall of 1900, at the age of 18, I was prepared to return to the University of Marburg, where I had enrolled in the spring semester. Suddenly I received notice that I was to serve in the German army. Since my parents were in a financial position to support me while in the military, I needed to stay only one year. The army installation to which I was assigned was located in Leipzig. By coincidence, a young German doctor, by the name of Grosse, with whom I had had a serious quarrel while at Marburg, was serving at the same installation. He and I were members of our respective university's dueling team, mine from Marburg and his from the University of Bremen. We had engaged each other in a dueling match which I won after an exchange not only of dangerous sword thrusts but also angry and ugly words.

"That evening, after the match, the students of the fencing society met in the university rathskeller to enjoy some beer and song. During the festivities, I went to the toilet. There I heard uncomplimentary and disparaging remarks not only about myself, but fencing teammates. The culprit spouting the most vehement words was Grosse. I was so angry that I walked up to Grosse and, without saying a word, slapped him across the face with my white gloves. Such a gesture was a disgrace to any young German who regarded himself a man, and Grosse left in a huff. Now, after almost a year, both of us were serving in the army at the same installation."

Henry looked intently at his hosts and continued.

"German soldiers enjoy their leisure time by drinking beer and singing martial songs in a place that serves good beer and has attractive young girls to enliven the evening. I was no exception, and I knew the hangouts. So did Grosse, and I ran into him again. Once more the ill feeling flared. Then and there we decided to end our feuding once and for all. No more threatening talk, but a dueling challenge for life, without any bodily protection and with specially honed swords. We agreed to fight in the vicinity of Leipzig. On the appointed day, early in the morning, Grosse and I faced each other. The battle line was drawn. This was for real. Our lives were at stake. During the fighting both of us were seriously wounded. Fortunately the referees stopped the duel, and both of us were taken to the hospital in the city of Leipzig. Grosse's life hung in the balance for three weeks. I was in for repairs to my chin which took a serious cut right down to my jaw bone. I also had a deep cut on my forehead."

Keyl had heard many scenarios, but he was not about to interrupt this one.

"My parents had the only telephone in the village. As soon as they learned that I was ill in Leipzig and had received permission to visit me, they rushed to the hospital. You can imagine their anxiety and then their shock when they entered my room. There I was, my lower jaw practically severed from my face, and my forehead with a deep cut. By hand signs, I assured them that I would be all right.

"After three weeks I left the hospital and was allowed a brief furlough. I must have looked like a military casualty to my brothers and sisters and friends when they saw me with my head so heavily bandaged. I remained at home long enough to recover completely from my wounds and then returned to Leipzig to complete my military service. In the meantime, the Grosse family in Bremen sued my parents for a sum of 2,000 marks, a small fortune even for a moderately well-to-do family. At the trial I was found guilty, and they had to pay. It was a hard pill for my father to swallow.

"After release from the army, I returned home to prepare for the continuation of my studies at Marburg. But my father had other thoughts, for I had flagrantly disobeyed his order never to engage in a duel for life. We left the rest of the family and went to the cellar to discuss the matter. Soon tempers flared, and it was clear that there would be no meeting of minds. My father disowned me and asked me to leave home immediately. Stubborn as I was, and with my pride deeply hurt, I accepted his ultimatum and told him that if he no longer wanted to accept me as his son, I would be ready to go out into the world and live my life without admitting to anyone that I was the son of Peter and of Katherine Nau. That very night I prepared to leave my home for good. It was a harsh decision, but I stuck to it. So did my father, and my mother tearfully faced the fact. As a parting act of love and concern, she gave me thirty marks and said, "Henry, spend this only in the greatest of emergencies." I said goodbye to everyone in the family and left my ancestral home. That was the spring of 1901. And here, a year and a half later, I am in the *Pilger Haus* in New York."

"How did you get here, Henry?" asked Keyl. Noticing the tired strain on the young man he did not press for an answer but urged his new arrival to have something to eat, take a bath, and prepare for a night's sleep. Henry did not forget Keyl's question. The next day he felt a bit more at ease and even found talking a great relief.

CHAPTER 2

"I told no one at home where I would go or what I planned to do. I became a wanderer, a prodigal, a man without purpose in life. Finally I settled in Monte Carlo. As many others had done, I decided to take a fling at life, and the devil reap the harvest. Dame Fortune was to be my counselor and my idol. I lived 'high on the hog,' and the gambling dens of Monte Carlo whetted my enthusiasm. I gambled not only with money but with life itself, and the goddess smiled on me. I won at the dice and roulette tables. With phenomenal luck I acquired a young fortune. Naturally I made many friends, among them two Americans.

"After my streak of luck, the Americans advised me to seek greener pastures in the gambling palaces of the Low Countries — in Bruges, in Lille, and other cities of Belgium. Luck stayed with me. Soon it was Paris. Money came and money went, and I enjoyed every minute of it. Thirsty for adventure, I could not wait to broaden my field of activity. My American friends urged me to come along to London. That was the place, they assured me, where I would really meet people who were willing to put everything on the roll of the dice, the fall of a ball, or the turn of a card. In London, as at Monte Carlo and the Netherlands, the goddess continued to smile on my profligate life. I never thought of home — at least I never wrote a line to let my family know where I was. I felt more and more that my responsibility was to no one but myself. I spent an entire year of my life in this frame of mind.

"In the summer of 1902 I accepted the invitation of my two American friends to sail for New York. The line was the same. In New York a man could make it big as a gambler. Anxious for adventure, without parental restriction, I came to the big city, and it was not long before my goddess stopped smiling. Instead of making it big, I lost everything, including my fair-weather friends. I could scarcely recall what had happened to me. My zest for life was gone. I was a stranger in a new land and in unaccustomed surroundings. Then, as I told you yesterday, I opened the door to your *Pilger Haus*."

Henry had told the ministers everything, except the fact that he had thought of taking his own life. That remained a secret.

Henry's conversations with Keyl and Restin lasted three days. The recital of his escapades was a trying experience for him, but the therapeutic effect soon became evident. During that time he felt a change of attitude toward life. He agreed to start anew, and expressed the desire to study theology and to prepare for the ministry. As Henry was to interpret later, God had assigned him a mission. Almost two years had passed since he put his hand to a pen to write a letter home. Now, at the insistence of Keyl and Restin, Henry wrote his parents to inform them of his newly found life, to express his apologies for past actions, and to assure them that he would see them again.

Home was Beltershausen since September 21, 1881, the day he was born. His birthplace was a farm community near Marburg on the Lahn River in the province of Hessen, Germany. Martin Luther, the Protestant reformer of the 16th century, had called this area "a piece of well-cured ham on a platter of green parsley." He referred to the red-shingled farmhouses of the villagers and the green fertile fields. Henry was the second child of Peter Nau and Katherine Hofmeister Nau and had five brothers and three sisters, the two youngest of whom he had never seen because of leaving home. His mother had inherited the farm when her father lost his life in an attempt to cross the Lahn at flood stage with his team of horses and wagon. Although she was a spirited and capable woman, the farm was in need of a strong man. She solved her problem by marrying Peter, a man of better than average height and physical strength. In the war against the French in 1870–71, he had served his country as a member of the cavalry.

Home for Henry meant a formidable farm operation with more than ten farm-hands caring for the fields, the cattle, the sheep, and the buildings. The building cluster was of sturdy and rugged construction. All sections were connected in the form of a quadrangle with a broad passageway leading from the village street to the courtyard. To the left of the passageway was the family dwelling. Then came the buildings housing the granary, cattle, sheep, chickens, geese, and the farm implements.

Home was the village church, known as the *Lichtern Kirche,* from the custom of the worshipers to bring candles for light and a bit of heat in the winter. Here Henry was baptized eleven days after his birth, with the minister entoning one name: Heinrich. He was not given a second name. The sanctuary of the church displayed the inscription: "Jesus Christ was sent for us by God for wisdom and for righteousness and for healing and salvation." These words flashed through Henry's mind as he wrote home and also took on special significance in view of his decision to study for the Christian ministry.

Home was the village school, where Teacher Emil Most taught the three R's and the commandment "Thou shalt obey." Since unruly conduct was punishable with whippings, the school children, all taught by Most in a one-room school, found a way to protect their posteriors. They would steal his whipping stick and then carefully weaken it by cutting notches. One thwack and it would break into many pieces. Henry did not fail to participate in such delightful pastimes. School attendance also called for church attendance. Teacher Most saw to that, and Henry would watch his father napping during the minister's long sermons.

Home was the occasion of Henry's confirmation in Marburg, in 1895. It was a memorable day, for now he became a member in good standing of the State Church, the *Landeskirche.*

As Henry continued to write, he remembered home as the place where people believed the wisdom of the proverb: "Seedtime and harvest on Hessen Land are a duty given by the hand of God, who lends the bread and the fruit and adds the gift of sunshine at the right time." Home could be friendly or cruel. He recalled his friendship with a village shepherd boy to whom he had given a suit that his parents had bought him. For this deed of charity he received a strong admonition from his father. Henry called it "the million-dollar whipping." He also recalled the false charge leveled by villagers that he had a love affair with a village girl and had fathered an illegitimate child.

Home was adventure and daring. At harvest time Henry hitched old experienced horses with untried colts in the traces and drove furiously to the orchards to bring in the fruit. In the maddening ride he invariably lost more fruit to the farm road than he brought to the floor of the granary. He cared less for the loss of fruit than for the dashing thrill of breaking a young colt.

Many other memories flooded Henry's mind as he wrote his parents of his newly found vocation. Having studied at Marburg, he recalled that home also was a historic area of Germany that had much to do with the Order of the Teutonic Knights, with the Miracle of the Roses, and with Saint Elizabeth, the patron saint of the Hessians, the Thuringians, and the Hungarians — bloodlines that went far back into the eastern area of the Occident. He remembered that Marburg was the locale where Luther, Zwingli, and other reformers had engaged in memorable disputations that shaped the history of Europe for centuries. All of these kaleidoscopic scenes brought tears to his eyes and homesickness to his heart. Should he stay in America, or should he ask his parents for money to come home?

When he discussed this with his two hosts, Keyl and Restin, assurances from them made Henry's decision easier. He could enter Concordia Seminary located in St. Louis, Missouri, and prepare for ministry in the Lutheran Church. But it would be almost a year before he could begin his studies. In the meantime he had to find work if he were to stay in New York. He could not stay indefinitely at the *Pilger Haus*.

Through a New York employment agency Henry took a job in a hotel shoveling coal for furnaces which heated the rooms and lobby of the building. In his off time he frequented barrooms to drink beer and meet people. Among them was an Austrian ex-cavalry officer with whom Henry developed a close friendship. At times he was captivated by some who urged him to get with it and forget about becoming a man of the cloth. He still had the wanderlust but, when he wrestled with his conscience, he knew he had had enough of the profligate life.

While in the furnace room of the hotel, Henry dreamed of days gone by on the farm. He had worked from sunup to sundown in the fields harvesting the grain and had really enjoyed it; he was cut out for that kind of labor. Grandmother Bodenbender, also his godmother, had been his greatest benefactor. She had tried to make his preadolescent years more pleasant by taking him with her to the city frequently. Now he was sweating in the coal dust, hating every minute of the dirty and grimy work. "Something has to be done," he said to his friend. The ex-cavalry officer needed no second invitation to join Henry in a return trip to the emplovment agency.

The agency informed them that cotton pickers were needed in the fields of Virginia. They agreed to take the jobs. Transportation was to be provided by the hiring company. The *Pilger Haus* had been Henry's home for about a month. He thanked his benefactors and took off with the Austrian ex-cavalry officer by bus for Meherrin and its vicinity.

On the way Henry questioned his decision to prepare for the ministry. It ran through his mind again and again. He spoke more about his past life to his companion, who in turn shared much of his own. Most of it had to do with school and army experiences.

Peter Nau had not wanted his oldest son to follow in his footsteps as a farmer. The work was too hard. Since his son learned well and enjoyed it, he arranged to have Henry enter the gymnasium, the German equivalent of high school and the first two years of college. Henry first attended the one at Mannheim and later switched to the one in Marburg. He concentrated particularly on the study of classical languages and literature. He enjoyed reading Homer in Greek and reveled in the epic poet's recitals of heroism and valor displayed in the Trojan War. The Romans likewise intrigued him, and soon Henry was completely enamored of Greek and Latin. At the same time, he learned of Gordon of Khartoum, a famous military and political figure during England's domination of Egypt. The life of this soldier and statesman impressed the young Henry. Gordon's love and concern for disadvantaged and oppressed people touched something deep in his soul. At seventeen, in 1898, Henry passed his examinations to continue his studies at the University of Marburg. His personal interest was medicine, but his mother persuaded him to study theology.

Henry's life at the university was typical of any German youth who was privileged to attend such an institution. He lived with a family named Textor, at 30 Green Street. He did well in his studies but enjoyed fencing most of all. Concentration on the sport soon made him the natural choice for captain of the fencing team. He also joined the Marburg Teutonic Student Group, a fraternity of fencers who were studying theology. Despite his father's prohibition against participation in the sport, Henry could not leave it alone. A professor who knew of Henry's love of the sport spoke with his parents and finally obtained permission for their son to participate, with the proviso that he was never to accept a duel outside of his university activity.

His sister, Ella, once came to visit him while he was studying at the university. Henry knew of her coming and also of her fear of fencing. He prepared to play a practical joke on her at his Green Street quarters. Before her arrival he covered his face and arms with bandages to give the impression that he had been seriously hurt in a duel. When Ella entered the room and saw her brother in bed covered with bandages, she was frightened and urged her brother to stop the nonsense of fencing. He then revealed the ruse and convinced her that he should engage in the national sport. Even the girls loved a student who showed marks of heroism in dueling.

As their bus rumbled through the hill country of Maryland into the Tidewater area of Virginia, Henry continued to regale his companion with the story of his life. While serving in the Army as an infantry officer, lieutenant rank, he learned of the need of German officers in the African Cameroons. He wanted to go, but his mother dissuaded him. Later on officers were needed in China to protect German interests during the Boxer Rebellion. Henry volunteered but lost his chance by one lot. He even harbored the idea of joining the French Foreign Legion but on second thought felt that no true German could or would join such a rebel group.

On arrival in Virginia, Henry and his friend were hustled to the fields to gather in the remnants of cotton. Most of the fellow pickers were Blacks. Now, for the first time in his life, he heard the wail of the black man and saw his sufferings firsthand. He witnessed the injustices that arrogant white superiors inflicted on disenfranchised and uneducated blacks. This picture he never forgot, and the experience affected him deeply.

Picking cotton was no child's play, and the two young men, long accustomed to harvesting wheat, rye, and oats, soon talked about finding a better way to make a living.

That meant return to New York, with them paying the fare out of their own pockets. Once back in New York, Henry went to the *Pilger Haus* to visit his friends. He had not forgotten them or his promise. But he had to find employment.

Henry waited and prayed, and soon his future brightened. He received an offer to work on a thoroughbred-horse plantation, located near Wheeling, West Virginia, and owned by a Pittsburgh steel millionaire. The Austrian ex-cavalry officer agreed to join him in the venture. Once again Henry said goodbye to Keyl and Restin, who reminded him to be sure to enter Concordia Seminary. Henry promised that he would. It was now winter, 1902. Leaving the *Pilger Haus,* Henry and his Austrian friend went to Grand Central Station to catch a train for Wheeling, West Virginia, with fare paid by the agent who hired them.

CHAPTER 3

As the train carrying Henry and his Austrian friend chugged toward West Virginia, a vendor came through the coach and offered each occupant a chocolate bar. He did not ask for any money; he simply threw a bar into each person's lap. Henry had never experienced anything resembling such American generosity. Not having eaten much candy in his life, and always hungry, he ate the chocolate bar with immense relish. But his delight was short-lived. The vendor, who only a few moments ago had thrown the candy into his lap, saw the empty wrapper and asked for his money. To his chagrin Henry learned that everything in life carried a price tag.

The train rumbled on with the two passengers who were to live together for a period of nine months of the year 1903. Finally the conductor walked through the coach and called out, "We're approaching Wheeling Junction!" Henry had studied Latin. Knowing very little English, he understood that the word "junction" meant a coming together. He reasoned that this was the place to get off and find their destination, which was located somewhere outside of Wheeling.

After the train left, the two helpless travelers were surprised to find themselves abandoned in the darkness. No city was in sight. What should they do? One thing was certain. They could not stay where they were. They would have to find Wheeling. The best way to do that would be to follow the railroad track, so they made the final stretch of the journey on foot, a method of transportation to which Henry was no stranger.

In the early morning hours they reached Wheeling and inquired about their new place of residence. Learning that the plantation was a goodly distance outside of Wheeling, they decided to spend the rest of the day and the night in the town. When night arrived, they looked for lodging. Henry remembered hearing that German immigrants were proprietors of barrooms in America and the barrooms were always lighted by a single electric light outside. Henry saw a light in the distance and encouraged his doubting companion to walk in that direction. They arrived at a store which served, besides other commodities, beer. They ordered beer and asked for directions. Informed that their destination was still a good way from where they were and realizing that it was very late, they accepted the invitation of the kind proprietor to spend the night with him. Henry fell asleep that night eagerly looking forward to the experiences of the new day. They were to arrive at the plantation on the morrow, where Henry thought he would be doing the kind of work he loved to do back home in Beltershausen.

The next morning Henry and the Austrian awoke, dressed, came downstairs, and saw a table on which a very tasty breakfast was laid. Hungry as they were, both sat down, ate the breakfast, and then looked for the proprietor and his wife. When they neither found nor heard anyone, they decided that they had better be on their way. Acting as though they had been entertained unawares by angels, à la Hebrews 13:2, the two guests departed without leaving so much as a nickel for their breakfast. Finally, filled with uncertainties about the new venture that awaited them, they arrived at the plantation.

A new life now began for Henry. He was accustomed from his years at home to hard work and long hours and he tackled the farm work with joy and determination. It was regular farm-hand work, with special emphasis on cattle and horses, many of them valuable thoroughbreds that required a good number of workers. These workers lived in regular wooden barracks and ate in a common dining hall.

The quality of Henry's work soon became apparent to the superintendent of the plantation. He was impressed with the young German's determination and his ability to relate well to his fellow workers. Henry was a realist, yet with a streak of the idealist. He was an attractive lad, husky, weighing 200 pounds, and standing a little over six feet. The scar said something about his past life, but Henry had in no way played havoc with his health. He was strong mentally and physically.

Days passed, and he met the daughter of the superintendent. In time she fell in love with him and he with her. They talked about marriage. It was a chance of a lifetime for Henry. Not only could he have a fine wife, he could look forward to becoming a superintendent and ultimately gain wealth and position. But what about his mission? He had to face the inevitable — either to accept the young lady or to fulfill promises made to Keyl and Restin and to himself that he would study at Concordia Seminary. It was a hard decision, but finally he became convinced that he could not consider marriage at this time. It would not contribute to the fulfillment of the mission to which, he felt, God had called him.

Henry lived with ten men dormitory style. The food was nourishing but nothing exceptional. The beds, arranged in two rows of five each, left much to be desired but were serviceable. Henry began to have his doubts about the cleanliness of the place, especially when it interfered with his rest. One night something bit him. He turned on the light, examined his bed, and found, of all things, bedbugs.

In the morning he went to his superintendent to inform him of the problem. The superintendent told him that this was an occupational hazard at the plantation, nothing to worry about. He gave Henry some fluid and told him to apply it to his mattress. Such treatment, he assured Henry, should solve the problem. At the end of his work day, Henry did exactly as he was told. That night the same thing happened. Quite clearly the superintendent's remedy had failed. The uninvited guests were back having another free meal at Henry's expense.

Again he went to the superintendent, who sent him off with the same instructions. Henry concurred, but with some doubt about the effectiveness of the suggested treatment.

This time Henry got no sleep whatsoever, and his patience ran out. He roused the dormitory population and announced that the matter of bedbugs would find solution on the morrow. During breakfast, he asked his friends to meet him at the bunkhouse after work just before supper time. He would then demonstrate a remedy for the situation that had robbed him of two nights' sleep.

Without saying a word to his superintendent, Henry proceeded to take care of his chores. After his day's work he returned to the dormitory and overheard his companions whispering to one another in small groups. What solution did their bunkmate have in mind? Without a word, Henry went upstairs to the bedroom, opened the window, took his bed apart, grabbed the mattress, threw it out of the window and sent the bedstead after it. He then went downstairs, took a half gallon of kerosene that he had procured during the day, poured it over his bedstead and mattress, and set it afire. As the bonfire merrily burned itself out, he turned to his companions and glowed, "This is the only way I know of doing away with the problem." When the superintendent learned of it, he was angry but had to admit that it was undoubtedly the most realistic way of eliminating a problem that had been annoying not only Henry but also the other residents.

Henry and the Austrian often worked side by side and lived in the same bunkhouse. Even though they no longer shared the same objectives in life, they remained friends. One day the Austrian came to Henry to borrow three dollars. Henry was no easy touch and with some hesitancy he consented to lend the money, with the understanding that he was to be repaid on payday. Two days later Henry learned that his friend had left the premises to find work elsewhere. With him had gone the three dollars. Henry stewed about this for some time, for the three dollars was a tenth of the amount his mother had given him when he was asked to leave his father's home.

Three weeks after receiving the bad news, he went to the superintendent to request a day's leave. He had learned from one of the workers at the plantation that the cavalry officer was working at a nearby coal mine driving a wagon. Getting his Saturday leave, he set out to collect his three dollars. As he approached the coal mine, he saw a team of horses pulling a coal wagon coming toward him. The closer it came, the more certain he was about the driver's identity. When he was near the wagon, Henry cried out, "Halt!" The Austrian stopped his team. "I want my three dollars!" Henry demanded.

"I do not have your three dollars."

Henry repeated with louder tone and greater determination, "I want my three dollars!"

Again he received the answer, "I do not have three dollars to pay you."

With extraordinary agility for a big man, Henry jumped up to the driver's seat, grabbed the whip out of the hands of the Austrian, and threatened him with a good whipping if he did not pay him the three dollars. Realizing that Henry meant business, the Austrian reached into his pocket, took out an old billfold, counted out three one-dollar bills, and gave them to Henry, who returned the whip, jumped off the wagon, and said, "Thank you and good-bye." The Austrian drove his team down the road; and Henry, whose strong will and determination would later prove both a help and a hindrance, whistled to himself over his successful collection of a debt.

Days at the plantation in Wheeling passed rapidly. Winter gave way to spring, spring to summer, and only too soon the day came when Henry had to bid good-bye to his life in West Virginia. He packed, thanked his coworkers, said his farewells to all, and in September of 1903 arrived in St. Louis to become a student at Concordia Seminary, located in those days on South Jefferson Avenue.

He approached his studies with zeal and dedication and had no difficulty with his course work, since many of the lectures were given in Latin and German, the languages familiar to him. Whenever a course was offered in the English language, he had problems but he would not quit. One night he was in his room studying the English dictionary. A fellow student thought it was an odd way to learn a language but had to admire the spirit of a man who felt he could learn a foreign language by memorizing the dictionary.

The seminary's small enrollment of forty to sixty students — all male — made close relationships between students and faculty members an everyday experience. Among the professors who especially influenced his life were Franz Pieper, George Metzger, George Stoeckhardt, and Paul Bente. Henry kept strictly to business, the study of theology, and developed little social life outside the seminary. He spent most of his leisure time, enlivened with beer purchased at a local tavern, with fellow seminarians — George Schimmel, John T. Mueller, George Mennen and John Moebius — with whom he developed lasting friendships.

In the summer of 1904, after completing his first year of study, Henry was sent to Vennedy, Illinois, for a bit of practical experience in congregational work. He would never forget the circumstances of his arrival.

Henry had gotten into town very late in the evening. The Pastor and his family had retired for the night, and Henry feared to awaken them. He located the church building and decided to spend the night there. After trying several doors, he found the rear door open, went in, and made his bed on a front pew. He noticed a strange odor, but was too tired to worry about it. Soon he was fast asleep. The next morning, awakened by the crowing of roosters, he learned to his surprise that he was not the only one to sleep in the church building that night. Nearby was a member of the congregation who was lying in state in the church sanctuary. Henry was learning to live in the simultaneous presence of life and death.

During his brief stay in Vennedy, Henry received ample training in preaching, teaching, and making visitations. Again he met a young lady of whom he thought a great deal. It was another love affair that would put still another resolve to the test — whether to serve in the United States or to serve in India.

The inspiration of serving in India first came to Henry in his early days at Concordia. He developed an interest in giving his life as a missionary to the "deprived and lost peoples of the subcontinent." He realized that there were millions without the knowledge of the God who gave him and other believers meaning and mission in life. More and more he became convinced that God was calling him to that part of the world.

With his heart now set on India, Henry abandoned his love for the young lady. About the same time he joined the Lutheran Church-Missouri Synod as a full-fledged member and late in August returned to Concordia Seminary for his final year of study.

Although half a continent and a mighty ocean separated him and his parents, Henry worked out a reconciliation with them by letters, which now arrived regularly at the farmhouse in Beltershausen. At the same time, Drs. Franz Pieper and Louis Fuerbringer of Concordia Seminary had written to Henry's parents assuring them of his changed life and preparation for the ministry.

The two professors had also written Henry Stallmann, Sr., a graduate of Concordia, now serving a congregation of the Free Church of Germany in Allendorf, not affiliated with the State Church, about the Nau family. He made the thirty-mile trip to Beltershausen to visit them. This visit of a pastor from the church body which Henry had joined in America changed their lives. They not only became members of the church at Allendorf, but worshiped regularly each Sunday by traveling the sixty miles in a surrey drawn by a fleet footed team of roans. As a special thank offering for their son's new life, as well as for their own and that of the entire family, Peter and Katherine paid the entire cost of redecorating the church.

Their change in life style and church affiliation soon spelled tribulation for the Naus. The villagers of Beltershausen resented them for having left their church in the village to join a strange group in Allendorf, and feelings of estrangement rapidly developed into ostracism.

CHAPTER 4

Henry was fast approaching his last weeks of study. With each passing day he became more anxious to taste the real work. Finally, at Concordia Seminary's graduation ceremonies in June, 1905, he received his diploma and an assignment to India. He was ordained and commissioned at St. Andrew's Lutheran Church in Detroit, Michigan. Many wondered what precise shape God's mission would assume for this eager, now dedicated young theologian, trained, educated, and poised for India.

He left immediately for Germany to visit his people whom he had not seen for four years. While on the high seas of the Atlantic Ocean, many thoughts went through his mind. God, he realized, had been good to him. The only way, he felt, that he could give thanks was to fulfill his avowed mission. He was grateful to everyone who had been his inspiration during the two years at Concordia. Yet what about his coming reunion with his parents? He had an inner longing for it, but how would it all turn out? India! He was a single man, 25 years old. He had had his share of varied experiences, but would he fit into the situation there? Faced with such uncertainties, of one thing he was sure — God who called him to this very mission would not forsake him but use him to inspire others. Henry was coming home in good spirits.

No one was on hand to greet him as his ship docked at Bremerhaven. After passing customs, he traveled by train to Marburg, where a servant of the farm met him to travel the last few kilometers by surrey. It seemed strange that his parents weren't in Marburg to greet him. On arrival he learned why. He received the sad news of the death of one of his sisters who, on the day of Henry's arrival in Marburg, died of scarlet fever. The family was filled with mixed emotions — joy because Henry was home; sadness because Katherine was dead. He embraced them and shared with them his joy and his sorrow. On the next morning he attended her funeral.

Henry felt at home in Beltershausen. During his stay he pitched in wherever he was needed and made every effort to become better acquainted with his brothers and sisters. He met old friends and made new ones and revisited the University of Marburg to relive some moments of yesteryear. Nor did he neglect to revisit the humble village restaurant and bar in Beltershausen.

Near the end of his stopover in Germany, Henry attended a conference of the Free Churches in Niederplanitz near Chemnitz. He wished to meet fellow ministers and lay members of that group affiliated with the Lutheran Church-Missouri Synod. One of the interested laymen attending the conference was August Hempfing, the father of two teenage daughters, Ella and Helen. He was coowner of a textile industry in the city of Chemnitz, a devout, energetic churchman, and a leader in one of the congregations there.

Hempfing's daughters were very excited about attending their first church conference. All of the meetings took place at Zion Church, pastored by Otto Willkomm, who had served as missionary in India. They learned, as did all members of the conference, that a newly commissioned missionary to India, Henry Nau, was present and was to preach at one of the afternoon services. The girls urged their father to allow them to attend the service.

Helen was deeply impressed with the young missionary, and she felt a particular urge to do everything possible to remain at the conference for its duration. Her father and mother received an invitation from Katie Willkomm, the daughter of the host pastor, to come with Ella and Helen to an evening meal at the Willkomm home. Unknown to Helen, Henry had also received an invitation.

That evening Henry and Helen met but there was little opportunity for them to speak to one another. Helen consoled herself with the fact that the conference still had some time to run. "We've got to stay through tomorrow," she pleaded with her mother. "Tomorrow is wash day!" came the crushing and inflexible answer. Helen put up a fight to stay, and finally her father intervened.

During the night with the Willkomms, Helen needed no dreams as she thought of the young man whom she had met and whom she secretly liked a great deal. The next morning, Helen arrived at the church and saw Henry and his friend, Goodsman, chatting together. Unaware that he was being overheard, Henry was asking Goodsman whether he knew the Hempfing girls. After receiving an affirmative answer, he urged Goodsman to introduce him formally to Helen. Goodsman readily obliged. Henry's first meeting with Helen was brief, but auspicious. At that moment two hearts fused into one. Helen and Henry fell in love. It was the beginning of a whirlwind romance.

Since German custom did not allow a young lady to visit her intended at his home before engagement, Henry left for Beltershausen by way of Chemnitz to ask for her hand in marriage. Their engagement was announced on August 9, 1905. After this happy event, Helen, accompanied by her sister Ella as chaperone, visited Beltershausen to meet Henry's parents and his family and to enjoy a few days of companionship. They walked through the countryside as lovers do and visited the beauties of the Frauenberg. Much of their conversation was about India. Someday, and both hoped it would be soon, they would be together in that strange oriental land.

Unfortunately, they had not reckoned with ecclesiastical bureaucracy. Immediate marriage was out of the question, for the Foreign Mission Board of Henry's church had the policy that in the case of a married couple the man went to the foreign country first, and later his wife or his betrothed followed. It was thought that one greenhorn should go first, not two. Helen, though deeply in love with Henry and wanting to be constantly at his side, submitted to the arrangement, even though it meant a year of separation. As for Henry, he was determined to turn his span of loneliness in India into an asset. Once there, he would prepare for Helen's arrival and make all the necessary arrangements to ensure a wedding that would be suitable for a young European lady.

Before his departure, Henry enjoyed another visit with Helen in Chemnitz and preached at her home church, the Church of the Trinity. After that, on October 11, 1905, he left for India.

From Genoa, Italy, Henry sailed for southern India. As the ship moved through the blue waters of the Mediterranean into the narrow passes of the Suez Canal, with the towering pyramids of Egypt on one side and the desert areas of the Sinai Peninsula on the other, Henry looked forward even more keenly to the work and adventures that awaited him. Apart from what he had read in books during his term in St. Louis, India was still a land of mystery to

Henry. From missionaries' descriptions he knew that he would be entering a land beset at that time under British rule with poverty, full of endemic disease, often ravished by virulent epidemics, subject to the capriciousness of the monsoon rains, and served by agonizingly slow means of transportation. Only a year earlier a cholera epidemic and a bubonic plague had ravaged the very area of South India to which Henry had been assigned.

The Persian Gulf now came into view and Henry's mind recited once more the ecclesiastical decisions that had helped to alter his life's direction so radically. In 1893 the Lutheran Church-Missouri Synod had decided to make Japan its first foreign mission field. Among the members of the Missouri Synod's Mission Board at that time were C.M. Schwan and J.F. Zucker. Both of these men had been missionaries to India under the direction of the German-based Leipzig Mission, but had shifted their allegiance to the Missouri Synod in 1876. Schwan and Zucker helped formulate a plan that called for a young Japanese national, Henry Mitsuno, who was preparing for the ministry at Springfield, Illinois, to return to his homeland to begin mission work after the completion of his studies. But the beginning of 1894 suggested a change in plan. Theodore Naether and Frederick Mohn, two members of the Leipzig Mission Staff, were unable to work effectively with their colleagues because of doctrinal disputes. After being dismissed they made contact with members of the Saxon Free Church. Receipt of this news in January 1894 prompted the Missouri Synod's Board of Missions to hold the plans for Japan in abeyance. At a special meeting in Fort Wayne, Indiana, on May 1, 1894, both mission fields received scrutiny. A decision to ask the president of the Missouri Synod, Heinrich C. Schwan, to contact the districts for their approval to transfer the site of the first foreign mission field from Japan to India received favorable response. Naether and Mohn were invited to come to America. In the late summer of 1894 they arrived and successfully passed a doctrinal colloquium. After their acceptance, the two men received and accepted calls as missionaries to the first foreign mission field of the Missouri Synod. The commissioning service was held at Immanuel Church, St. Charles, Missouri. A former Indian missionary, C.M. Lohn, preached the sermon. President Schwan then gave a brief address and explained the circumstances of the day's events. He defended the defection from Leipzig by Naether and Mohn, and explained the Board's decision to enter India instead of Japan. On October 14, 1894, Schwan said:

> Very well. We take them and send them back again to the millions. We are certain and say clearly, "This is God's will and God's guiding." We are not sending them to the territory where they can interfere with the congregations of the Leipzig Mission, much less of any other heterodox mission. On the contrary, we have instructed them to begin in a place that is as far away from Leipzig Mission stations as possible.

The truth was that Naether and Mohn on their return to India, were met on January 20, 1895 at Tuticorin by John Kempff, a missionary in the Shevaroi Hills, located in the northernmost part of the Salem District in South India. Naether tried to find a station that would meet the requirements of the Board's instructions; yet the first station, while far removed from a Leipzig mission, was still in the vicinity of the Leipzig Mission interests in Krishnagiri, which was roughly one hundred sixty miles west of Madras and some sixty miles from Kempff's plantation. It was a strong Hindu and Muslim concentration. A few Roman Catholics, but no other Christians, were in the area.

While the ship was sailing through the Persian Gulf and the Indian Ocean, Henry read in a report that the children of Naether had died of the bubonic plague and were buried on the mission grounds at Krishnagiri. Even Naether had died of the plague, February 13, 1904. Numerous cemeteries claimed one, two, or more of a missionary's family.

Henry knew that his willingness to go to India carried a tag with a large price. He had grasped much intellectually, but the school of experience would exact its own toll. Cultural isolation would be a major factor in the adjustment to be made. He must learn a new language and different dialects, completely different even in thought patterns from those of his native tongue. He had been told that Indians frequently interpreted frankness in word and deed as boorishness. He had heard of Indian politeness and obliquity of speech and it would take some adjustment not to interpret them as deceit and duplicity. It would take a long time to understand that "next week" repeated two or three times was a polite way of saying "no." Western gestures of affection were often revolting to Indian society. Some of the amenities of Indian society would seem crude to a Westerner. He knew in his mind and heart that he was in for the struggle of his life to find a place in the approaching kaleidoscope of language, culture, and economics. Yet the challenge was itself an invitation.

He recalled how Christian missions began in India and pondered on their merit, their failures, and their successes. Henry was well aware of the tradition that ascribed the beginning of Christian work in India to the Apostle Thomas and his successors, but he also knew that history focused on the arrival of Vasco da Gama, on the Malabar Coast, May 20, 1498. The Portuguese introduced their religious customs, and colonists from other parts of the world brought their varieties of belief. In 1706 Bartholomaus Ziegenbalg began a Lutheran mission in Tranquebar, located in southeast India. William Carey pioneered for the English Baptists. Anglicans also enjoyed prestige. The differences among Indian Christians were indeed many. Roman Catholics experienced repeated jurisdictional disputes, and their debates with the Syrian Christians were well known.

Despite so much ambiguity in Christianity's impact on India, Henry looked forward with highest expectation to his assignment. He would work in a land that had millions of people, most of whom were Hindu, a large percentage Muslim, and less than two percent Christian; and most of these were not in the area of India to which he had been assigned. He was aware that progress in Christian mission work would be desperately slow. Yet, despite such negative considerations, Henry welcomed the moment to go to work. Nothing deterred him, not even the news that the bubonic plague in the area assigned to him had dropped the statistic of baptized members of the Lutheran Mission in Krishnagiri from forty-five in 1901 to thirty-eight in 1904. Deep in thought and prayer, he arrived at Colombo in Ceylon. There he was greeted by George Naumann, a missionary with whom he was to work in Krishnagiri.

CHAPTER 5

Henry had no doubts about the warmth and sincerity of George Naumann's welcome. Mother nature's hospitality was another matter. As both ate breakfast the next morning in a Colombo hotel, a flock of crows flew into the dining room through an open window and in one swoop cleared the table of all edibles. It happened so quickly that both Henry and George scarcely realized what had happened. If this was the first installment of nature's reception to this part of the world, Henry wondered what other surprises were awaiting him.

Later that day they traveled by small craft to Tuticorin. Once in India, they traveled by train to Krishnagiri, a town of 8,856 population, due west of Madras, the capital of the state of Madras. For a time Henry made his home with the Naumann family. They lived in a house constructed of kiln-burnt brick, laid up in mud and plastered over with lime and mortar. It had a red-tiled roof. The kitchen was outside of the house. The living quarters consisted of two bedrooms, a study, a parlor, and a large back porch. Flowers and rose bushes lent a pleasing appearance to the exterior of the home.

Henry spent much of his first year learning Tamil. He could not work with the people until he spoke their language. Every day he applied himself to a task that he relished. Language study was his hobby. Besides German, he had developed varying proficiency in English, Swedish, Dutch, and Norwegian, and he was familiar with Greek and Hebrew. In the process of acquiring Tamil he conversed in German or English with older fellow missionaries and nationals. His progress in Tamil was so excellent that local people would say, "This one speaks our language."

Aggressive and resourceful, Henry brought to the mission field a revitalizing spirit. His experiences with common people in Europe and America stood him in good stead, and colleagues observed that he adapted very readily to the ways of the people of Krishnagiri and its environs.

The Krishnagiri mission numbered only thirty-eight baptized members, and these were mostly of the economically and socially depressed class. The missionaries lived in a compound separating them from the squalor of the villages and towns. Such an arrangement was not the best for contact with the people. Henry soon felt this alienation. To overcome it he went out every day to the villages and fields where the people lived and labored and spoke with them. He had a pointed message for anyone who would listen. On one of his many trips he saw a man patching a roof.

Henry asked him, "What are you doing?"

"Patching the roof," came the reply.

"Why are you patching the roof?"

"It might rain."

"Yes, it might rain someday. So also with you. You need patching."

After he had caught the man's attention, Henry told him how God in Jesus Christ had come to patch his and everyone's life.

A missionary's daily activities called for flexibility, and Henry was prepared to meet the demands. He spent many hours helping sick people receive assistance for diagnosis and care at government hospitals. He counseled with families that experienced problems occasioned by the caste system. The fact that he was a Christian and not a Hindu also could spark social repercussions for people who associated with him. Wealthy landholders would not take kindly to missionaries who met socially with sweepers or coolies. Henry himself had no problem. He visited the dwellings of the impoverished and the "palaces" of the rich. He was as much at home in rice paddies as in the pretentious homes of landowners. To outcaste as well as to the highly respected Brahmin, Henry brought the same attitude and the same message. He was convinced that everyone was in need of the good news, the opportunity of the second chance in the forgiveness of sins earned by a suffering and dying Savior and the expectation of a better life, the new life in the power of the Spirit of God and in the joy of loving and serving one's fellow human being.

Henry readily accepted invitations to eat with villagers in their homes. Although the diet of Indians differed from that to which the newly arrived missionary had been accustomed, he readily adapted to the cuisine. Like most visitors to India, he soon learned to enjoy Indian curry. "The spice of the gods," he called it. He would sit with his host on the naked ground in lotus fashion, the customary posture of people in India as they dine. In front of him and each of his companions, who sat with him in a circle, was a banana leaf. In the center of the circle was a large pot filled with the curry sauce and fish. Rice, in one form or another, was eaten at almost every meal. At any feast rice was heaped on several banana leaves next to the pot of curry. Knives, forks, and other utensils were lacking. Everyone used his hands to make small rice balls, sticking them on the small finger. They were then dipped into the curry sauce and deftly stuffed into the mouth. Dried fish was served with the curry, and bananas concluded the meal.

Most of Henry's daytime hours were spent in language study and occasional trips to the village and fields to engage the people in conversation about the Gospel. He would also visit the mission school. At night he reviewed his language exercises and wrote love letters to his Helen. His parents heard regularly from him about his activities. Knowing that Helen would join him at the end of the first year, he engaged local carpenters to build furniture and laid in store other household articles. Thirty dollars, his salary per month, did not stretch far, but his thrift made preparations for his marriage possible.

As his proficiency in the language progressed, he threw himself into the everyday labors of a missionary. Like most of them at the time, he was up by four in the morning and in his oxcart by six heading out for the rice fields. He spoke to anyone who would listen. Some conversations were friendly, others were heated.

Some things Henry learned fast, others more slowly. At times he knowingly acted contrary to the feelings of the people, so anxious was he to impress on them the message of God's love and protection and to disperse the fear they had of their gods. In such frame of mind he visited the Hanuman temple, revered by worshipers of the monkey god, Hanuman who, according to the Indian epic, saved Rita from her kidnappers to unite her with her lover, Sita. Everyone coming to the temple removed his sandals to approach the sacred area in bare feet. All, except Henry. Immediately he was surrounded by a boisterous, angry mob which demanded that he be punished. He talked himself out of this dilemma but learned a lesson he would never forget. While disagreeing with the beliefs and actions of the Hindus, he must have more respect for people and their religious beliefs, customs, and traditions.

In addition to his daily contact with people in villages and fields, Henry wrote simple Bible stories, which would then be taught by local teachers to the school children. On Sundays he delivered sermons. He attended conferences with lay workers and fellow missionaries. Despite his distaste for paper work, he prepared reports regularly for the superintendent of the Mission Board in the United States. At the end of the day, tired but optimistic, he slept on a cot covered with mosquito netting. This protected him from mosquitoes as well as vermin that had their habitat in the rafters of the mission house.

CHAPTER 6

Henry's immersion in his work helped the year of the separation from Helen pass more quickly. For Helen, his bride-to-be, it was not so easy. Absence from her beloved was hard to bear. She used much of the time to prepare for her long journey to India, where she would meet her fiance and be united with him in marriage, but still the days passed slowly. Finally, the eventful moment came. It was time to leave Chemnitz for Krishnagiri. Her parents traveled with her to Genoa, Italy. After a tearful good-bye, she boarded the steamer for her voyage to India, accompanied by the missionary family of George Kellerbauer.

Henry met her in Colombo, and together they traveled the same route Henry had taken a year before. At last they were in each other's arms. Henry, who had waited with longing heart for her to share his labors and to establish their own home, rode the crest of happiness. As for Helen, Henry's every wish became her command.

November 12, 1906, was their wedding day. Henry, 25, and Helen Carolina Bertha Hempfing, 21, were united in holy matrimony in the Evangelical Lutheran Chapel in Krishnagiri, Salem District of the state of Madras, India, with George A. Naumann, Henry's missionary friend, as the licensed clergyman performing the ceremony. Witnesses were many, but only George O. Kellerbauer and Albert Huebner signed the marriage certificate.

During the ceremony, the Indian children of the mission school sang in German *Jesu geh voran auf der Lebensbahn,* ("Jesus lead us on the path of life"). As Helen heard the song sung by Indian children in her mother tongue, she cried. The marriage and the wedding dinner, held in Naumann's home, gave a clear picture of the psychology of the Lutheran missionaries working in the Indian field. They were all of German descent and, consciously or unconsciously, imposed their cultural thinking on the lives and ways of the people with whom they worked. A missionary's success evidently depended on his ability to Europeanize Indian Christians.

During his preparations for the wedding, Henry had spent many days planning not only those matters that pertained to the ceremony itself, but also the events that were to follow. Forty-five guests, including twelve Indian flower girls dressed in white, attended the wedding feast. Two days of work went into the preparation of the feast, with everything under Henry's supervision, including the butchering of a heifer. Rice and curry with all the trimmings were now served, and merriment continued into the night.

In 1907, two years after Henry's arrival in Krishnagiri, word came that a second field of mission activity was to be opened at Nagercoil in the state of Travancore, at the very tip of southern India about 400 miles from Krishnagiri. An Indian, Ganamuthu Jesudason, had sent a report to the Mission Board in the United States urging extension of the work of the Lutheran Church-Missouri Synod, in India. Jesudason was a Christian from relatively low caste. Having been educated to the university level and employed by a British officer, he was cognizant of developments of foreign missionary enterprises. He approached the missionaries of the Lutheran church in India to take over the independent congregation of which he was a member.

The missionaries moved in. Located 400 miles south of the Ambur District, the new field became known as the southern field. The Ambur area, the first locality in which the missionaries of the Lutheran Church-Missouri Synod had worked, was known as the northern field. Both were, of course, located in South India.

In the judgment of the missionaries it seemed that a stricter adherence to caste laws was evident in the southern field than in the northern. The Shanar, or Toddy drawing caste, and the outcaste Puleyas maintained varying degrees of isolation from the high caste Brahmins. Until 1854 the Puleyas were virtual slaves. The fact that they were released from slavery at that time had not ameliorated their condition to any great extent. They still lacked many political and social privileges, and some of them were looking to the Christian mission for escape from entrapment in their caste systems. Missionaries might have thought that their adherents were motivated by purely material considerations, but acquaintance with the Christian message had bred hope within some of these poor people, and they ventured to request aid from the mission.

Among the requests was one made by Jesudason. He wrote to the leaders of the church in America:

> I am glad to report that the German branch of the Missouri Evangelical Lutheran Missionary Society has kindly granted permission to their mission-aries to start Christian work in Travancore, one of the important protected native states in India. At present the work will be confined to Vadaseri, one of the suburbs of Magacora, the chief station in South Travancore where an independent congregation of about 160 souls exists. I mean a congregation quite unconnected with any recognized mission. In course of time we can move to the heathen Panchama villages in South Travancore.
>
> In December last, 1906, I wrote to one of the missionaries, the Reverend H. Nau at Krishnagiri in the Salem District, appealing for spiritual help in behalf of the heathen Panchamas of South Travancore, who, according to the census of 1901, number nearly 30,000 in six taluks, meaning counties. Two of the members, the Reverends A. Huebner and G. Naumann, were deputed to proceed to Travancore with a view to learn whether the condi-tions were favorable for doing evangelistic work there. On the 21st of February, 1907, they arrived at Magacora. I accompanied them to several heathen Panchama villages.
>
> While at Magacora, the pastor of the independent congregation ap-proached the missionaries and personally expressed a desire after due consideration with his flock to entrust the congregation to the missionaries. . . . In due course permission was granted by the latter home board to their missionaries in India to take over the independent congregation and also to commence evangelistic operations among the heathen Panchamas of South Travancore in July last. This time for the purpose of finding out what the objections of the London Missionary Society were. And if they had any real objections, how far they could be recognized. On his return to Ambur, a conference was again held in which it was finally decided to undertake work in South Travancore.

On March 5, 1908, Henry and Helen had their first child, a boy, whom they named Walter Theodore. Now the work demanded that they leave Krishnagiri and move to Coonoor, where on March 26, 1909, was born their second son, Eric George. Helen kept watchful eyes on her children, assisted by faithful Indian ladies serving as Ayahs. These servants were a standard part of the economy and social structure and in keeping with the recognized status of the white man as part of the ruling establishment at that time.

Henry had been in the Ambur District for almost four years when word came that he should go south to Nagercoil, twelve miles from the southern tip of India, Cape Comoria. The transfer, in late 1909, brought a fresh challenge. He now had to learn another language: Malayalam.

Numerical growth in the mission came much more rapidly in the southern field of the Lutheran Mission. A superficial reason was the shifting of allegiance from the London Mission, or the Salvation Army, to the new mission. More important was the fact that the London Mission Christians had gone through decades of persecution from Hindu neighbors and had finally hewn out an arrangement by which they could follow their faith without undue harassment. This benefited also the outcast communities that wished to become Christian. In this way the Lutheran missionaries were able to reap the results of others' labors.

While the family lived in Nagercoil, another boy, John Fredrick, was born on October 8, 1910. Although infant mortality ran very high in this part of the world, the family, especially Helen and the boys, enjoyed good health. They counted this a special blessing from God. In spite of the humid heat in the dry season, they remained hale and hardy. Henry did not fare so well. Because of his arduous activity and willingness to eat all kinds of food in all kinds of places, he contracted bleeding dysentery and a touch of malaria. He steadily lost strength and weight and during the nine years of labor worked himself from 210 pounds to 165. He sported a handlebar moustache, which contributed to the drawn appearance of his facial features. The more weight he lost, the more prominent the moustache appeared. While attending the first conference of the northern-southern fields in Krishnagiri, Travancore, in 1912, he appeared to be in poor health, yet his spirits never flagged.

During his stay in Nagercoil, the problems of caring for his family multiplied because of the cholera epidemic that raged throughout the villages surrounding Nagercoil. Normally the family got their drinking water from the village well and ran it through a porcelain filter. But even this process did not encourage potability during the epidemic. The result was that the entire family, including all children, thought it best to live on coconut milk for a period of six months, and the family survived without serious illness.

In 1912 Henry moved again — this time to Trivandrum, another town in the southern field, about 50 miles northwest of Nagercoil. There Helen gave birth to her first daughter, Esther Frieda. The London Mission, which was already in the area, was not pleased, but concluded that there was little point in protesting Henry's arrival. Their objections to the Lutheran Church-Missouri Synod's intrusion had already failed in 1907.

Henry was recognized from many directions as a capable worker, but not everyone shared his conviction that the Lord approved of such aggressive action as he had evidenced in the move to Trivandrum. Nor was his board in St. Louis pleased to learn that Henry had undertaken mission work in a new area without permission on their part. In his report to the board, Henry had also chided its members for their indecisiveness and for lack of confidence in the actions of their men in the field. Director Julius Friedrich, aiming to cool off a somewhat heated correspondence, wrote in reply:

> I plead with you, my dear Brother Nau, as your friend and as a friend of our beloved mission, try with God's help to be more restrained in your writing. Such explosions are an excessive burden to me and to other friends of mission work.

Responding specifically to Henry's unilateral action, he continued:

> Just as I, while eagerly awaiting your answer, had built up a singular enthusiasm, even a previously unimaginably foolhardy enthusiasm for Trivandrum, your stream of cold water came. If this matter had not already been decided, I doubt whether it would have come through in its present form.

The move to Trivandrum was bound to expose some of the problems confronted by workers within India's caste culture. At the time of the move, several men of the area demanded that the Lutheran missionaries work exclusively among the Sambavars, a low-caste people, for the first fifteen years. This request must have puzzled the missionaries, for in the group making the demand was a man of mixed caste, J. Canchanam. The missionaries refused to restrict themselves but did begin work among the low-caste people who had invited them.

Trivandrum also provided opportunity to work in another language, Malayalam. To Henry's way of thinking this meant further extension of the gospel. What he failed to take into sufficient consideration was the vast effort required just to prepare textbooks, catechisms, and hymnbooks in a new language.

Frederick R. Zucker, who had begun the study of Tamil but diverted his efforts to Malayalam, joined Henry in Trivandrum. These men were in turn joined by John C. Harms in 1912 and Otto A. Ehlers in 1913. The arrival of August J. Lutz to Nagercoil in 1912 gave both Trivandrum and Nagercoil a full complement of workers and noticeable impetus to the mission.

The work, as all mission work in India, was still painfully slow but showed further signs of acceleration after the resolution of some especially volatile sources of contention. In the early days of the Lutheran Church-Missouri Synod's work in India difficulties in communication among members of the mission staff were minimal. The missionaries labored in only one field, and since most of them were from Germany they knew one another rather well. Even those who came later were of German descent and had been educated at the same seminary in St. Louis. There was little that could bring about a difference of opinion or promote unusual friction. But expansion of work in two different districts made some personality clashes among the missionaries inevitable.

Correspondence from the Mission Board to the field in 1910 and 1911 expressed alarm at a rift that had developed between the two districts. At issue was the allocation of missionaries. There was great joy in the United States in early 1912 when a one-word cable arrived from the field: "PEACE." But it was only a truce. Another bone of contention developed somewhat later when missionary Ehler's assignment to the northern field was shifted to Trivandrum.

Henry's decisive initiative while impatiently waiting for orders from headquarters in St. Louis undoubtedly was a contributing factor to the friction that occurred between Henry and the board. Yet there were practical considerations that could not always wait for bureaucrats' decisions. Primary in Henry's judgment was the purchase of a place that would permit the missionaries to enjoy a suitable climate during their vacation periods. For a long time missionaries had agitated for a mountain home in Kodaikanal. In the plains during the dry season, the temperature would often rise to unbearable heights with almost 100 percent humidity. Neither children nor adults could escape severe cases of prickly heat and boils. Some relief was available for brief periods of time in rented quarters that the missionaries used for hill leaves, but the facilities were quite inadequate, and parents were forced to send their children back to Germany or to the United States at the age of ten or twelve years in the interest of health as well as education. Extreme heat like that in South India was not conducive to the full mental development of a Caucasian child.

While Henry worked in Trivandrum, prior to and during the first general conference of Indian workers, Superintendent Julius Friedrich made a visit to India. The missionaries' request for a mountain retreat had been going unheeded, and Henry was determined to broach the subject afresh now that Friedrich was in the area. The opportunity came when Friedrich visited with Henry and his family. While eating supper, the superintendent removed his sun helmet. Shortly after the meal he became nauseous and retired to the bedroom. Troubled about his illness, he asked Henry what the cause might be. Henry, anxious to make his point about the need of a vacation home in the hills, admonished Friedrich: "You're lucky it's only a slight thermal attack. Never take off your sun helmet, not even indoors!" Without hesitation, the superintendent promised his help to make a summer home possible.

With the help of the Walther League (a young people's group in the United States affiliated with the Lutheran Church-Missouri Synod) and the women of churches in the United States, monies were gathered to purchase a summer home in Kodaikanal, an important hill station located roughly between the two districts in South India. Kodaikanal was on top of a range of mountains 7,000 feet above sea level. The mountains, known as the Palni Hills, were geologically old and resembled the Appalachian Mountains of the eastern United States. Hill station sounded like a misnomer, but in the land of the Himalayas, 7,000 feet was not a great height. Similarly, the plains were incorrectly named. In Indian missionary English, the point of demarcation between hills and plains was one of climate, not elevation.

In honor of the seller, whom Henry remembered only by his family name McNair, the property was named Lochend. It consisted of three acres of land with two double residences. The cost of the property was about $9,000. Immediately after the purchase of the property, the missionaries requested $2,000 for building an additional vacation residence. The monies for this residence came from a Walther League society through the encouragement of the Rev. Oscar Kaiser of Milwaukee, Wisconsin.

With the purchase of the hill property, the question of allowable duration of hill leave arose. In 1899 the policy had been a three-month leave every three years at the missionary's own expense. In 1912 the time had come for a new policy. The missionaries in the field suggested a leave of two months every two years. Henry had something to do with the new arrangements. "One who works hard has also the right to play hard" was his philosophy.

Getting to the hill country was not easy. As Henry described it:

> At night we went to the backwoods dock in Trivandrum and boarded the boat that was pulled up to Quilon. It took all night to make that 50-mile trip. The next morning we took the train from Quilon to Kodai Road. That took all day for 130 miles. We got off the train and onto a bandy (oxcart) for the 25-mile trip to Periakulam. That took all night. Early the next morning coolies came along and took our luggage on their heads, and others took Mrs. Nau and the children in palanquins and carried them up the mountainside. They would have taken me, too, but the swaying of the palanquin always made me sick, so I walked. As we walked up the mountains, the weather became cooler. At five in the evening, we would be in Kodai.

In 1912 trains and buses replaced boats and oxcarts to bring people to the foot of the mountains, and promises were made that a motor road would be opened up, replacing the ten-mile coolie mountain trip.

Henry's mission obligations kept him constantly on the move, yet he found time to continue his study of Tamil and Malayalam. Intrigued also by the "holy language" of India, Sanskrit, he delved deeply into the literature written in that ancient tongue. Combining his intellectual interests with love for people, he took the time in 1912 to write about the area of Travancore and the city of Trivandrum. He entitled his book *Vanji Bhumi,* that is, "Place of Love," or "Chamber of the Sweetheart," published by Concordia Publishing House in St. Louis, Missouri. In keeping with the Pauline model of becoming all things to all men, Henry identified more and more with the people of India. He sat square-legged among them on the floor. He gesticulated like them in conversation. He ate their food and even drank their water.

Henry did most of his traveling on horseback. It was the mode of transportation to which he had become accustomed in Germany and on the plantation in Virginia. Jim, his horse, was very tractable, with one exception. Having been accustomed to life with a rice farmer, Jim loved to bathe himself in any water hole at any time, especially in the heat of the day. During the dry season, no matter how urgent Henry's business was, Jim would look for a water hole, and no matter how sternly Henry tried to prod him away from the water hole, Jim, who shared his master's temperament, subbornly moved toward it in order to cool off. Henry was forced to sit with both his legs under his body on top of the horse's back while Jim was totally submerged in water with only his neck and head sticking out. Such equine behavior gave Henry trouble, but instead of stewing over it, he decided to do the same as Jim and took a quick bath in the water hole.

On one such occasion, he was with a fellow missionary worker. Both of them decided to join Jim in his ritual. They undressed, laid their clothes on the bank of the water hole and took their baths. Washed and refreshed, as fully as that was possible in a season of extreme heat, they returned to where they had left their clothes. To their surprise, their underwear was gone. They searched but did not find it. Fortunately, their shirts, trousers, and sandals were still there. Several days later Henry was in the village and solved the mystery. One of the villagers was wearing his underwear. Oddly enough, he was using the pants as a shirt and the shirt as a piece of loin cloth. Henry laughed so hard that he forgot to reprimand the boys who had temporarily caused him discomfort.

Other situations were not so laughable. Without the cobra India, especially in the southern part, is like Australia without the kangaroo. Henry and his family were not spared encounter with this venomous creature. On many preaching missions he visited native huts which had walls rising only several feet from the ground, with bamboo poles on each corner to hold the roof, which was constructed of palm branches and thin bamboo. One day he was in the middle of his sermonette when a cobra appeared and put on a dance in front of him. He stood amazingly quiet, fearful of moving even an eyelash. After looking at Henry for a while, the cobra slithered toward the lower edge of the bamboo roof to escape. Before it got away, several people, equipped with hoes and rakes, killed the reptile.

One afternoon daughter Esther, in care of her Ayah, or Nanny, was playing in the garden when suddenly a cobra raised its threatening head a mere two feet from her. The nurse, sensing the immediate danger, threw herself between the cobra and Esther. She jeopardized her own life but fortunately was not struck by the snake. None of the Nau family members was bitten by a cobra during their stay in India, and all of them discovered that snakes are actually quite timid and flee at the first sound or crunch of footwear on the ground.

Other undesirable creatures were encountered at times. Once Helen awoke to find a mouse nibbling on her toes. And Henry would find grass snakes coming into the house unnoticed, winding their bodies around kerosene lamps or lying in the moist area of the bathroom. But they provided only momentary chills.

Oxen could also be sources of anxiety. More dangerous in some ways than motorcycles, they could break away from their cart, with everyone running for life. After they had been quieted down and rehitched, no one was the worse for wear. On one occasion, however, Henry had hitched two oxen to a cart. The leather bindings worked loose, causing the cart to lurch. Eric, who was sitting in the cart, fell backwards. The accident caused a stutter that plagued Eric throughout his childhood.

Southern India was also the lair of the leopard. Early one morning the Nau's chicken yard had been robbed of all its flock. The gardener informed Henry that he had seen the paw marks of a leopard in the dust of the chicken yard. Henry and the gardener decided to give the leopard an unwelcome surprise should he return. For several nights they sat in the trees armed with powerful rifles. The scavenger did not appear. On the fourth night, shortly after twelve, Henry noticed two animals coming across the compound wall. Anticipating a great feast, they made their way to the chicken yard and toward the barn where two calves were housed. As soon as the leopards, a male and his mate, came in range of Henry's rifle, he pulled the trigger. He had shot his first wild animal during his years of service in India as a missionary. The gardener tried to get the female but failed. Henry did not have the prize trophy mounted. Instead he had the animal skinned and prepared for use as a rug, which graced his study for years.

Henry learned early in his Indian days that Hindus venerated all life, for all life originated with Brahma and returned again to Brahma. Letting of blood was therefore contrary to Indian belief and practice, but Henry never developed sympathy for life at all costs. Once an Indian python had devastated his chicken house. Called by the gardener, Henry hunted the monster and with the assistance of a number of Indian Christians killed it. To teach the Hindu villagers a practical lesson that they need not fear the wrath of the god Vishnu because of the killing of an animal, he had the dead snake placed on a board and carried by four members of the Christian congregation through the village streets. Undoubtedly many angry eyes pierced him, but he did not desist from carrying out the experiment. Whether this display of insensitivity to Indian custom accomplished its purpose history does not record. That he had not learned too well his earlier lesson in connection with the monkey episode is clear.

Henry harbored a keen interest in the daily occupations of the people. His missionary bungalow was regularly visited by Hindus who came to entertain, not only with their dancing cobras, but also with other tricks that were the stock in trade of itinerant entertainers. They were experts at releasing all kinds of rubber goods through their noses. These rubber goods resembled potatoes, eggs, carrots, and bananas. Physical deformities of the mouth and nose, such as harelip and cleft palate, could be put at the service of such performance. All in all, the entertainment was harmless and broke the monotony of the family's life.

Henry enjoyed supervising building operations. He was no contractor and had no experience as a carpenter, but he delighted in planning bungalows for missionary families. He supervised one in Nagercoil and a beauty in Trivandrum. His family never had the opportunity to live in the latter, but Henry was not disturbed: "I do not find it a problem, and I have no regrets," he said.

The principal difficulty plaguing the mission during these years was lack of money. In July, 1913, Henry received word from St. Louis that the house he was building in Trivandrum was too expensive. The letter read: "We must be very careful with our money; otherwise, a real deficit will flower."

"Members in the congregations in the United States are not working hard enough (for missions)," was the reply Henry expressed in an article published in his church's official paper, *Der Lutheraner*. In need of money, he had written the article without permission of the board. This they deemed poor judgment and insubordination. They were not pleased with his direct approach to the congregations, and they feared the repercussions of his criticism. Henry, on the other hand, was surprised at the board's reaction. Eager and anxious to go ahead, he felt that the kingdom of God was under no compulsion to be a respecter of statistics, monetary or otherwise. Needs were there to be met. The bungalow was needed for the mission and its missionary and therefore had to be built. Ways and means had to be found. Practical requirements took precedence over institutional ego.

As his nine years of Indian service came to an end, the statistics of the mission showed 675 converts compared to only 57 in 1907. He left India and its people reluctantly, but he needed a rest. His loss of weight and his bleeding dysentery required immediate attention. However, he planned definitely to return. It was to be only a furlough.

He knew that as a young man of action he had created ill will among some missionaries and some members of the mission board. It was a risk he had to take. If something had to be done, there was no time to wait, and God would forgive.

CHAPTER 7

On April 7, 1913, Henry and the family sailed from Colombo, Ceylon, on the North German Lloyd steamer, *Kleish*. It was a day of mixed feelings. Farewell to India, if only for the duration of a furlough, was not easy, and there were important items to take care of in the interval.

High on the list was a visit to a doctor to check out his physical problem. Another was a visit to the United States to lecture on his work in India so that more support, moral and financial, could be obtained. A minister, T. Harms of Bancroft, Nebraska, had invited him to speak to his congregation, and the Mission Board had arranged for a lecture tour, especially through the Midwest. He was to book passage on the *S.S. Berlin* and leave Germany on August 4, 1914, with arrival in New York on August 12.

Henry was most anxious to visit the States and eager to see his brothers, Peter and John Henry, whom he had not seen since 1901 and who, in the meantime, greatly encouraged by him, had come to America to study for the ministry at Concordia Seminary in St. Louis. Peter was serving a congregation in Ohio and John one in Wisconsin. The Missouri Synod's procedure called for Helen to remain in Germany. As the members of the board stated, "America is not the native land of Mrs. Nau. It were better she would not come."

The arrival in Chemnitz, Helen's home, was a memorable one for the Naus. Helen's father, mother, brothers, and sisters were at the railroad station to greet her, Henry, and their four children. For the first time the grandparents saw the children and were able to hold them in their arms. Everything portended a grand vacation. The reception was impressive. Grandfather August had a number of limousines waiting at the railroad station to take the family from the station to the home on West Street, where they were greeted by a firecracker display.

During the early months of the furlough, Henry visited a doctor, who immediately diagnosed his illness as dysentery. Ignoring Henry's pleas that the diagnosis be verified through an operation, the doctor wrote out his prescriptions. With medication, proper rest, and careful dieting, Henry was soon on the way to full recovery. Yet he never rested. He gave many lectures to German congregations, and whoever invited him received a pep talk on the thrill of foreign mission work in India. It was his life, and he held his audiences spellbound.

Only a few days remained before his sailing date on the *S.S. Berlin*. Suddenly war clouds gathered in central and western Europe; and on August 1, 1914, war was declared. This news was bad enough, but it also spelled ruin for his trip to the United States, for there were no visas to be obtained. Then, on August 4, the day scheduled for his departure for the United States, he received orders from the German government that his services were needed to repel the threat on both the east and west fronts. The German Reich had not forgotten that, despite his absence of twelve years from his homeland, he was still one of its officers.

With this traumatic change of events, Henry's life took on a different direction. India became a dream, and with it all that was left behind — friends, coworkers, people, even the possessions of the family. Henry had little time to ponder the sudden change in his life — from a messenger of peace to a man of war.

Ordered to appear at a soldiers' barracks in Chemnitz, Henry underwent a total transformation in a few minutes. He stood outside a building from which various types of army equipment were being thrown. Most of it was military uniforms. Knowing his size, he hunted in the stack of clothing for underwear, shirts, pants, coats, overcoat, and boots. He was now attired for service.

After assignment to a battalion, he was given a brief furlough to bid his family good-bye. He went home to take a last look at all his loved ones. The thoughts that passed through his and Helen's minds as they took leave of each other were inexpressible. Only three weeks before, on July 14, Mary Ann, the fifth child, was born into the family. Now he was telling Helen that he had a feeling he would never return from battle.

Henry made a strong and imposing figure in the gray of the German infantry uniform. Even though he was a minister and could have been slated for assignments other than the infantry, he considered it his duty to help protect his country and loved ones from the enemy.

Instead of serving on the Eastern front, his battalion was among the first to move through Belgium in the hot August days of 1914. He was in the very midst of the early fighting. Though spared injuries, he saw the naked hatred that was generated by the people as they faced each other in deadly combat. Women poured boiling water on the heads of invading soldiers. Rape and murder of civilians, as well as rear-guard action of the populace that claimed the lives of many of his comrades, were hourly experiences. He noticed retaliating brutality on the part of his own soldiers.

Moving through Belgium, they reached French soil. In the trenches he had a number of close calls with sudden death, but none closer than the one that took the life of a comrade. A captain of his battalion, whom Henry had befriended, was ordered to determine the position of the enemy across the lines. With rifle and binoculars in hand, he crawled over the trench to get a better view when suddenly the bullet of an enemy sniper hit the captain, piercing his skull. His body fell right at Henry's side. It did not move, and Henry knew his friend was dead. Death on the battlefield could be quicker than that caused by plague or cobra. He seemed to hear the strains of the soldier song, *"Ich hat einen Kameraden"* ("I had a comrade").

Henry was not afraid to die. He knew that his life was in the hands of God, for he had experienced many an incident in India that deepened his faith in the truth: "What happens must happen. It is the will of God." Henry believed more and more that man's destiny was determined by his Creator and his Redeemer. He was puzzled only at the panorama of life — from helping to save lives in India to killing men and destroying property in Europe.

Henry had opportunities for study while in the trenches. At times he read the Greek New Testament, one of a few books he had taken with him when he left home. His superior officer saw what he was reading. Not knowing the Greek language, he was surprised that a field-grade officer was reading a book with rather strange writing. He queried, "What are you reading?"

"I am reading the New Testament."

"Are you able to read it in that language?"

"Yes, sir. I studied Greek while I was at the Gymnasium, at the University, and at the Seminary in America."

"Then what is your occupation?"

"I am a minister."

"And you're here in the front fighting as a common soldier?"

"Yes. I felt it was my duty as a citizen of Germany."

"We'll see what will happen to you," the officer replied.

Fighting continued, but shortly after the conversation with his superior, Henry received orders to report to a large hospital located eight miles from Chemnitz. He was to serve as a medical chaplain. The new assignment brought him safely to Helen and the family. His fear of never coming home from war was allayed.

At the time Henry was very optimistic about the outcome of the war. German forces were moving successfully on both fronts, east and west, and he informed the members of the board in the United States that he felt the war would soon be won by Germany and that he with his family would be able to return to India. Reality, however, proved Henry wrong. The war dragged on, and the longer it lasted, the more ominous the days became for the German people.

Regardless of the tides of war, Henry worked with great enthusiasm as the appointed chaplain of the sanitarium. His family also grew in number from four to seven children — Mary Ann, Henry Richard, and Irene, all born during the war years. It was a challenge to keep the clan going and growing, and salaries were pitiful.

Every Sunday he conducted divine services. He made visitations at the bedside of the wounded and celebrated the Lord's Supper. As celebrant of the rite, he took the view that only those who understood what the Sacrament meant should receive it. It was a stance of conscience. He was convinced that communion involved both a blessing and a hazard. Therefore he required announcements prior to the communion service so as to have the opportunity to explain his position. After consultation, he permitted only those who were of the same conviction as he to receive the Lord's Supper. This was his belief, and he stuck to it. How he managed this in the imperial army of Germany remained a secret. How he harmonized such exclusiveness of the gospel in communion with his missionary spirit of inclusiveness also remained a secret.

He saw the wounded brought in by the carloads from both the Eastern and Western fronts daily. Usually, the doctors attended first those who appeared to be in critical condition and then the less severely wounded. One day Henry saw two men in the hallway. One soldier lying on the floor had received a very serious wound that had torn the lower part of his body into shreds. He was crying for water. Realizing that he had very little time to live, the orderlies brought him water, not in a cup or in a glass but in a bucket for, as he drank, the water simply passed through him. There seemed no hope of life for this man, and yet he continued to live in agony for some time. The other young soldier sat complaining of a headache. The doctors did not think he was seriously wounded and did not immediately attend to him. Suddenly the young man stood up, cried out, fell down, and died. The doctors were very much surprised and, after an autopsy, found a small piece of shrapnel at the base of the brain. How puzzling life really was, thought Henry, and how everything held on to a thread, broken only by the will of God, who had created it.

It was very fortunate that Henry's family had access to the mess hall of the sanitarium. This helped the family in its desperate need for food. He and the mess sergeant, who was his friend, arranged to bring two of the children at a time into the kitchen. He sneaked them in at various times to enjoy a good meal of noodle soup and prunes, potato salad and, of all things, a piece of fruit. These were delicacies for stomachs accustomed to a daily diet of rutabagas, brown bread mixed with ground cardboard, and potato peelings. Henry often obtained sausage and bread from the hospital commissary and under cover of darkness walked eight miles to Chemnitz and arrived at Kyffhaeuser Street. Knocking on the window, an arranged sign for Helen to know that Henry was outside, he handed her the supplies. Military orders forbade him to enter the apartment where his family lived.

Henry also managed to visit his father and mother, who lived in Wiesbaden. While Henry was in India, his father had sold the farm in Beltershausen and had moved to this resort area in the Rhine Valley. After several unsuccessful business ventures, he moved to a government property, Greenberge, raising and training German shepherds, which were being used as message and medicine carriers on the front. He tended a productive garden, raising potatoes, cucumbers, beets, carrots, and other edibles. Henry, in need of food for his family, would visit his parents during brief furloughs. Once, on his return to Chemnitz, he tried to bring back potatoes for his family. There were none to be had on the market, since all were requisitioned by the army. On departure from Wiesbaden, he took a suitcase, filled it with potatoes, and camouflaged it. He would have to pass inspection at Mainz. Choosing a time of traffic congestion to cross the bridge, he thought he could get by customs without detection. He was mistaken. To his chagrin, the inspector asked him to empty the suitcase's contents and confiscated all of the potatoes. Had he not been an officer, and a chaplain at that, he would have been fined also.

Near the end of the war, Henry and Helen, to make ends meet, had to send Walter and Eric to the grandparents in Wiesbaden, where they remained for the rest of the war. On top of hunger came sickness. Still an infant, Irene developed scarlet fever in the winter of 1918. The home was quarantined. In order that John and Esther might attend school during the quarantine period, they were sent to stay with Helen's father and mother. The same winter Helen, exhausted physically and mentally, contracted the swine flu and suffered a very serious case of pneumonia. She was at the point of death, and each night the family gathered around the supper table to ask God to heal her and keep her with the family where she was greatly needed. Their prayers were answered. God had more work for Henry and Helen in His mission.

The news that came from India was depressing, and Henry tried to help, but without much success. He heard that missionaries Albert Huebener, Reinhold Freche, Henry Stallmann and Jean Jacques Williams were in a concentration camp, while Mrs. Huebener with her four children sat alone in Kodaikanal. In a moment of desperation Henry cried out: "Until the war is ended! How will it then be with our mission field? Will the mission in India be in existence at all? Who knows! No question, we live in bad, bad times. God have mercy on us!"

Before the words escaped, Henry consoled himself with St. Paul's exclamation of hope: "In all these things we are more than conquerors through him that loved us."

CHAPTER 8

On November 11, 1918, the war ended. With no other work available and a family to support, Henry remained in the military for another year. It was a hectic one. Germany was in a state of confusion. Its military was weak and its economy worse. Saxony also experienced unrest.

Many advocated the Communist ideologies. Workers and soldiers who received a mere subsistence salary wanted to overthrow the government in power and to establish, if not a communistic state, a socialistic one.

Henry attended meetings of soldiers and workers, and when the question was asked who could handle a pen, he volunteered. When asked whether he spoke Russian, he answered, "No, but I can read it." Henry saw here the opportunity to wield some influence and to direct the actions of the people. He certainly wanted no strife or bloodshed. He had had enough of that. He did not want Chemnitz to be a battleground.

One thing was obvious, the men wanted more money. At the meetings were many big mouths who wanted to be leaders. They felt that by sheer volume of decibels and outshouting of the less vocal they could influence the people to select them as leaders. Henry, knowing something about the democratic process and the power of the ballot box as practiced in the United States of America, suggested that after due discussion a vote be taken on matters of jobs and salaries and that the will of the majority prevail.

To his surprise, after his speech he was elected president of the workers-soldiers organization of Saxony. Assuming his office, he quickly ordered everyone to remain calm, especially those in the military units and the hospitals. He then chose three members of the workers' committee to visit the Reich's treasurer in Dresden to negotiate for better wages for all workers and soldiers. He also looked forward to speaking to King August, ruler of Saxony. As the men neared Dresden, they heard that the treasurer had been murdered by a Dresden mob and thrown into the Elbe River. King August could not be seen. After such violent news, Henry and his colleagues returned to Chemnitz. From that time on he realized that it would be safer for him to relinquish his position as president. Convinced that fierce confrontation was not God's mission for him he quietly and determinedly gave more authority to fellow officers of the workers' organization and slowly worked his way out.

His income at this time amounted to 525 marks a month, of which 330 came from Lutherans of the Saxon Free Church, and 195 from two German friends, Arthur R. Ahrendt and Paul Heylandt. In addition he received 75 marks per month from the German government for military service; these he returned to the church.

What Henry did from 1914 to 1919 was, so far as he was concerned, simply a bad dream. He had been decorated with the Iron Cross First Class for bravery and faithful service but showed it to no one, not even the members of his family. He worked toward his doctorate in Sanskrit Literature and received his degree from the University of Leipzig, Halle, on January 28, 1920. The cost of his dissertation (*Prolegomena zu Pattanatu Pilaiyers Padal*), paid by the Lutheran Church-Missouri Synod, was 2,600 marks. However, he never called himself "Doctor", but signed all correspondence with a simple "H. Nau."

Uppermost in his mind was the mission in India. Throughout the war he had maintained contact with the Board of Missions in the United States. When all else failed, he went through the Consulate of Denmark. At the conclusion of the war, he learned with deepest regret that because of his German nationality he was not allowed to return to India. This was a bitter pill, and he decided to get back the hard way, by becoming a citizen of a country that would make it possible for him to return. That country was the United States. However, the members of the board in America now looked at Henry with different eyes. Some of them questioned the advisability of bringing to the United States a man who had seven children and a wife to support, without the prospect of employment. Henry learned of this attitude and, without registering disappointment, continued his efforts.

Shortly before Christmas, 1919, he received a call to the pastorate of Holy Trinity Church in Berlin. This required a move for the family, whose very departure for Germany's capital was inauspicious. On boarding the carriage with her children, Helen dropped her sewing basket. As the contents spilled to the floor of the carriage, Henry was heard to mumble, "This is typical of my family — all of its earthly belongings in a small basket now spilled on the floor."

Shortly after his arrival in Berlin, he learned that there was room for a missionary in China. He wrote the board in the States about his willingness to go but learned that the board considered it advisable to send a man who had a smaller family and had more medical training, a much-needed skill for work in China. Immediately, Henry dispatched a letter to the board, not rebuking its members for their choice, but expressing resentment over the fact that family statistics were a factor in determining eligibility for work in China.

Henry's stay in Berlin was brief — from October, 1919, to January, 1921. The Mission Board in St. Louis had changed its mind about Henry. On accepting the call to Holy Trinity, he had advised the members that he still harbored the desire to return to India. He also felt that the Armistice of 1918 had solved nothing and that war would come again. Therefore, when the invitation came from the United States, he accepted and made arrangements for the journey to the New World.

After 6½ hectic years in Germany Henry, Helen, and the family sailed on the *Susquehanna* from Bremerhaven for New York. The cost of the trip was financed by the Lutheran Church-Missouri Synod. The tickets amounted to $1719.06, with $50 for incidentals. Helen, for the second time in her life, left her homeland in tears. Again she followed Henry to a strange land, with a language and customs that were equally strange to her.

CHAPTER 9

The *Susquehanna,* a ship once owned by the proud German Navy but confiscated by the American government after the war, was the Nau's home for 23 days. The voyage was a stormy and adventurous one, with the family comfortably housed in two cabins. After seven years of hardship in Germany, the meals served in second class seemed a luxury. Henry asked and received permission to conduct Sunday services in the dining hall. On one of these Sundays, the storms were particularly vehement, but Henry delivered his message without loss of composure. The unusually bad weather forced the old ship, which was covered with ice, to make a non-scheduled stop in Boston before proceeding to New York City. She was about to complete another routine crossing of the North Atlantic, but for Henry and Helen it was a unique voyage and the beginning of a new venture.

It was now February, 1921. The last meal on board ship was at the special invitation of the captain. Henry, Helen, and the youngsters enjoyed another taste of good food before hitting the streets and skyscrapers that were Brooklyn, one of New York's boroughs. The dinner consisted of sauerkraut and frankfurters. The young ones were anxious to get a look at the streets, for they had been told before leaving Berlin that "gold lies on the streets of New York, because America is the land of material prosperity." There was no gold, but plenty of mud. The river front of Brooklyn had never appeared very hospitable, but it did point the way to freedom, opportunity, and peace.

Thirty-four-year-old Helen and her seven children faced a new life in a new country. For Henry it was a return to America and, he hoped, a chance to go back to India. He remembered that on December 29, 1918, he had written the Board of Foreign Missions:

> We are more than ever determined to serve our mission in India and pray fervently that our Heavenly Father may remove all the obstacles that block our way towards the work that is so dear to our hearts. At the same time we entreat you, dear fathers, to do everything in your power to open the roads that are now barred to us. We anxiously await the day that brings back peace to Europe and permits us to leave this country and [we await] our venerable home board to kindly take immediately every possible step at Washington and with the immigration authorities to be permitted to land on American soil where we are very eager to make ourselves useful. We request that some work be assigned to us temporarily until by the help of God we may be allowed to reenter our much cherished mission field of India. . . . The terrible war has left all of us practically untouched so far as our mere lives are concerned. In all other respects we feel the consequences of the war even more than others who are permanently settled in this country.

He had persuaded the board members that he was ready to go to any land and work in any language. Now he was in America. One fact was evident from his enthusiasm on arrival — he looked forward to his stay in America. He had no promise of work; he did not know where he would go. Yet he had in his mind and heart the hope that he would be busy in mission until he could become an American citizen and then return to his beloved India.

Coincidentally or otherwise, the Reverend Otto H. Restin, who had much to do with changing the course of Henry's life in 1902, met him on arrival in New York. Emotions ran deeply, but there was little time for them. The family had to go on foot, baggage and all, to New York Central Station, and Henry had to contact several friends in the city and members of the Mission Board. He also spoke by telephone to his two brothers, Peter and J. Henry. Peter had invited the family to come to Sherwood, Ohio, where he now pastored a rural congregation. Henry informed him that they would arrive in about 48 hours.

The train for Sherwood was scheduled to leave late at night, giving the family about eight hours to roam and play in the large railroad station. Instead of going to a restaurant or to some greasy hole in the wall, they ate their supper in the great hall — the waiting room of the railroad station. Henry had bought some bread and sausage. That was the menu for the evening meal. While eating, sitting on suitcases, the children were intrigued by the Red Caps, Negro porters, who toted the passengers' luggage. It had been a long time since they had seen a dark-skinned person. Whispering to their mother, they asked whether the men with black faces had failed to wash themselves. Their naivete was to be more forgivable than the actual prejudice and lamentable stupidity about other races that they would encounter in the 'Land of Opportunity.'

The family waited for the announcement to board the train for Ohio. When the time arrived, they entered the proper coach and settled down for a long ride. What they could expect was anyone's guess. Even Henry did not know what would happen. Fortunately his son Walter was born to be inquisitive. As the train raced through Maryland in the wee hours of the morning, Walter, who had learned a little of the English language from his father and from listening carefully to people on board the ship, heard the conductor announce that the train was on its way to Pittsburgh, Pennsylvania.

Walter ran to inform his father, who was napping on a seat of the coach. Henry made inquiry and to his chagrin learned that he and the family had boarded the wrong train — one going to western Pennsylvania instead of western Ohio. It was not Henry's fault, but the conductor's oversight when he took the tickets. About 4:30 in the morning the family shuffled off the train and found itself in the town of Cumberland, Maryland. The conductor made arrangements for them to stay in a hotel, where they spent more than a full day.

It was a seminar in shock for the parents. They had all they could do controlling the curiosity of their children. The youngsters pointed at every waiter in the hotel restaurant and, among other things, ate bananas, peel and all. Mercifully another train arrived and all were on the way to Defiance, Ohio, and Sherwood. The schedule of this train called for an early morning arrival in Sherwood.

It was long before dawn and no one was awake at the time to welcome the foreigners, not even Uncle Peter and Aunt Martha. After the train left, the family found itself in the wide open spaces in total darkness, not knowing where to turn.

Henry located the railroad tower, where a switchman was on duty. He climbed the ladder up to the switchman's roost, and there he found help to contact his brother, Peter, by telephone. He informed him that the family, the "German invasion," had arrived.

None of the kids dared to wander too far in the darkness after having been told that in America there were many deep holes, and if they were to fall into one of them, they could not be rescued. The boys, however, found the small wooden railroad station of Sherwood nearby. They pried one window after another and finally found one unlatched, opened it, and heaved each member of the family into the inviting railroad station, heated by a well-stoked coal stove. The wintry weather and snow-covered ground were not very hospitable that early in the morning, and they were all glad to be indoors. After being in the building a while, Eric discovered that the door could have been opened from the inside and everybody could have walked through the door instead of being pushed through the window.

While the family waited for Henry to return with the good news that Peter was on his way with horse and wagon, the children discovered a machine containing chewing gum. Not knowing what chewing gum was, but anxious to try some, they received several pieces by dropping pennies in the money slot. It tasted like candy and a real treat which they proceeded to chew and then eat.

Finally, in the early hours of a February morning in 1921, Henry, Helen, and family arrived at the home of Peter and Martha, which was to house them until other accommodations were located. Peter and Martha had their own family. For a time things were very pleasant; Henry and Peter talked unendingly about the past. They had not seen each other since 1905, sixteen long years. Martha and Helen also got along well, but Helen knew that two families cannot live under the same roof peaceably for any length of time and she was anxious to have her own home. Things became especially difficult when Henry received orders from the Lutheran Church-Missouri Synod to make himself available for lecture tours. This meant that Henry was on the road most of the time from February through May, and Helen was left with the care of the children. Walter was immediately sent to Fort Wayne, Indiana, to start his preparation for the ministry. He was not able to speak English fluently, but most of the instruction at Concordia Junior College was in the German language. Several times Walter ran away from the school to return to the family. Homesickness was a terrible experience, and Concordia was not the most desirable school for a foreign boy to make a transition to a new life.

Henry's family of seven children related only too well with Peter's four. All of them had to sleep in the attic on simple pads. It was a great place for wrestling matches, which disturbed everyone and especially Aunt Martha. Also, many of her superb apple pies, baked every Saturday morning and placed on the window sill of the kitchen to cool, disappeared. The culprits were Eric and John.

The straw that finally broke the back of domestic coziness showed up in the classroom of the church school. John, with his inquisitive mind, dared to ask his uncle, who was not only a minister but also teacher of the church school, what one meant by "ding-dong-ding-dong" as they prayed the section of the Lord's Prayer that went, "Thy kingdom come, Thy will be done." Such a sacrilegious question did not go unpunished. After a severe tongue lashing and a hefty spanking, he was dismissed from school. He told his mother that he would never return to that classroom. His brothers and sisters agreed with him.

The relationship between the brothers' families was becoming more and more strained.

When Henry came home from a lecture tour, Helen urged him to arrange for a move, not only because of the children, but also for her sake. She had her problems with Martha. At last a farmer offered his barn to house Henry's immigrant family. Farmer Jost became a good friend of the family and enjoyed having the children around. The "farmhouse" was more suitable for rats than for two-legged creatures, but a stranger never asks the details of an act of charity; he accepts the hospitality. That was Henry's philosophy.

All in all, life as lived by the family in that first American house was not unbearable. In the daytime the children had fields to roam, creeks to fish, and eggs to find. And at night the rats entertained the children with their acrobatics on the barn floor. The unevenness of the floor made cooking a real problem for Helen, but she managed and never complained.

Since the older children were not attending school, on one of his rare visits home Henry arranged for them to attend a country school located about three miles from their home. He assured the boys that the teacher spoke German, which, of course, was of great comfort to them since they had their difficulties with the English language. Henry knew he had to use this as a ploy to get them to go. Eric, John, Esther, and Mary Ann were enrolled and every day hiked six miles during the latter part of the winter and the spring of 1921 — three miles to the school and three miles back home. They did not mind the walking, for they were accustomed to that from their days in Germany. Unfortunately, they were not received kindly at this school, where they learned that the teacher did not speak German. Finally, when John was hit by a schoolboy with a rock and in reprisal stoned a suspicious-looking schoolboy, the teacher quickly called Eric and his sisters into his office and told them to pack their books and leave the school. That was the tragic end of the second school experience of Henry's and Helen's children in the New World.

In May, 1921, Henry received a call to teach at Luther College in New Orleans, Louisiana, more than 1,000 miles from the place where they had come to make their first home. It would be his responsibility to help prepare black boys for the ministry and black girls for the teaching profession. A doctor of philosophy in the Sanskrit language, a philologist of no mean reputation, a man of wide experience in world missions was called to teach subjects in arithmetic, civics, catechism, and other high school subjects. On December 12, 1918, he had written that he "would be ready to go to any land and work in any language." India remained uppermost in his mind, but at this time in his life Henry's mission was in New Orleans and he accepted the call.

Henry and Helen were glad to tackle their new venture. They arrived in New Orleans in the summer of 1921 and began life in the Crescent City on the banks of the mighty Mississippi River. Besides being one of America's most interesting cities, New Orleans had a climate that reminded the Naus of the humidity and heat they had endured in India from 1906 to 1913. It was a slight bridge to the past.

Luther College was located on Derbigny Street near Annette. The school was founded by the Reverend Frank J. Lankenau in September, 1903, in the small pastor's room of St. Paul's Lutheran Church. Lankenau served the institution as president and professor until September, 1908. He also served the congregation, a small black group, as its pastor. Reverend Gotthelf M. Kramer, superintendent of the Louisiana field, was likewise connected with the early years of Luther College. It was a small operation owned and directed by what was called The Synodical Conference, of which the Lutheran Church-Missouri Synod was the greatest moving force in association with several other Lutheran groups.

Henry's family was quartered in a residence on Thalia Street, located in a residential area of the lower-middle-income class. Superintendent Kramer had made the housing arrangements. The house was more of an apartment, with no room for play indoors or outdoors. Henry knew it was no place for his large family. The first thing he did was search for more suitable living quarters. He did not know very much about New Orleans, but he knew people, and after a brief stay on Thalia Street he located a rather comfortable half-house through the efforts of a newly-found friend. The rental fee was the same as for the apartment on Thalia Street. The dwelling was located at 324 Hagen Avenue, better known as Jefferson Davis Parkway. It was a modest house with five rooms, a bath, a small porch, and a small backyard. In New Orleans slang, it was a shotgun house. Especially attractive was the fact that it faced a double thoroughfare with a large grass area between the roadbeds. The area in between was called by the children of the neighborhood "The Green." The street, covered with oyster shells, extended from the new basin to the old basin, two waterways which were in operation between the lake and the heart of the city. Here at 324 Hagen Avenue, Henry and Helen made a home for the next four years.

Life for Henry meant work at Luther College. Graduates of the school went to Selma, Alabama, an academy for Blacks, or to the seminary, also for Blacks, in Greensboro, North Carolina. All three institutions were supported by the Synodical Conference of the Lutheran Church.

Hugo Meibohm, who subsequently became Henry's personal friend, was the president of Luther College. The other men on the all-white faculty were Walter Beck, a very energetic young man whom Henry liked very much, and a clergyman, Erich Wildgrube.

Owing to the small faculty, Henry had the opportunity to teach almost any subject. This leeway he enjoyed. His morning schedule called for the following: At 8:45 A.M., a chapel period of fifteen minutes. From 9 to 9:40 A.M., a bit of American, European, and church history. Arithmetic was scheduled from 9:40 to 10:20 A.M. Henry had never received any special training in teaching arithmetic, but he convinced his family that he could add five and five. From 10:35 to 11:20 A.M. the students were taught pedagogy. Henry must have smiled to himself the first time he announced this subject to children who hardly knew what the word "money" meant, much less "pedagogy." Another horrible name, physiology, was used for simple, ordinary, everyday biology, taught from 11:20 to 12:00 noon. Following a forty-five minute lunch break, the afternoon schedule called first for catechism (that is, Luther reedited), from 12:45 to 1:25 P.M. Much of the work was in the form of memorization by the student, with simple explanations offered by the instructor. General history from 1:25 to 2:05 P.M. gave Henry the opportunity to talk about anything that interested him. Increasingly he loved his work among the Blacks, but India was constantly on his mind and he talked a great deal about his experiences there. Because of its importance to future teachers, pedagogy came up for a second round, from 2:05 to 2:45 P.M. He had no opportunity to teach language, literature, or the practical approach to evangelism.

While in New Orleans, Henry received a call to Buenos Aires, Argentina, to occupy a professorship at a Lutheran seminary. For the first time in their lives together, Helen made the decision. With tears in her eyes, she informed Henry that if he wanted to go to South America she would not stand in his way, but she felt that he ought to stay in the United States. She had come this far with him, and now she believed that this was the land for her children. Henry listened, and at that moment the tables were turned. Her wish became his command.

Six times a week, morning and evening, from September to the end of May, Henry walked to Luther College. It was a good three-mile walk from Hagen Avenue to Annette Street. He loved it. Not only was he saving money, of which he had very little, but he needed the physical exercise. One night, homeward bound, the wooden plank spanning a gutter broke, and he fell into the open drainage ditch. He was covered with mud and human and animal excrement. He also caught a cold, one of the rare ones of his life.

Because of his energy and broad interests, he took an active part in the larger work of his church in New Orleans. He was interested daily in telling the message of God's love in Jesus Christ. This fervor for evangelism brought him to the attention of the Mission Board of the Southern District. Gottfried Johann Wegener was president of the district, and he saw that Henry had the ability to speak to ministers and to lay people alike about their responsibility in sharing their faith with other people and not to hide it under a bushel. Wegener asked Henry to serve in the mission efforts of the district, an invitation that he accepted readily.

Henry worked so spiritedly in district activities that his zeal came to the attention of the faculty. In October, 1924, the Secretary of the College directed a letter to the Southern District with the complaint that the district's work was consuming too much of Nau's time. Henry did not mind the work. However, according to the minutes of January 2, 1925, a resolution was passed which read as follows:

> The president of the Southern District shall be notified by the secretary that we are forced to complain to the Southern District because of the burden of duties placed upon our Dr. Nau by said District. At present he holds four major offices with them and finds that his efficiency is impaired because of the same. We shall request that he be relieved of all these duties at the next synod meeting in February of 1925.

Whatever these four major offices were is not recorded in Henry's correspondence or in the records of the Southern District, but his most active office was certainly that of mission director. He made visitations throughout Louisiana and southern Mississippi, with occasional trips into Alabama, to encourage the young pastors and lay people to be more active in the work of the mission. He never mentioned to any of his friends, not even his fellow faculty members at Luther College, that he regarded this work as a burden or that it in any way impaired his efficiency as a professor. Even his service at St. John's Lutheran Church on Canal Street as vacancy pastor, after the death of Pastor Julius Friedrich and before the installation of Pastor Martin W.H. Holls, in no way impaired his duties to Luther College. In fact, Henry was known to open the day at Luther College almost regularly, for he was a stickler for getting the day under way on time. Hugo Meibohm often came to the college too late to do the honors appropriate to his presidential office. Henry inspired the student body and encouraged the faculty to be filled with the same spirit. He carried a full teaching load every semester. In his last semester at Luther College, in 1925, he taught civics, catechism, school management, general history, and pedagogy — a full complement of classes augmented by many hours of personal counseling. After eighteen or more hours at the college, he came home very late at night. In view of such dedication to his immediate responsibilities, he could not understand the feelings of the faculty concerning his extracurricular activities.

What did depress him at times was the appearance of the paternalistic attitude of the men charged with supervising the operation of the school, namely the superintendent of the Louisiana field, and the Mission Board of the Synodical Conference. Many of the boarding students slept in double beds, and the facilities were not what they should have been for a reasonable life style. Secretary Edward Stoll reported that "the faculty considers the double beds in the boys' dormitory undesirable because of their moral and hygienic danger, also because of their present filthy and dilapidated condition."

The school operated on a shoestring. Even the visit of a representative of the board did not ameliorate conditions. Their complete misunderstanding of black people led to heated discussions. The faculty of Luther College saw the handwriting on the wall, and conditions deteriorated to the extent that even the requisition of a new typewriter became a major issue. "Since the typewriter at present in the office has outlived its usefulness," Stoll wrote, "it is resolved to ask the honorable Board to permit us to hand it in for another." In all of this, Henry was a willing combatant. More than ever he was convinced that the practical aspects of mission work must be supervised by people who were engaged in it on the field and not by men meeting in executive conferences and general assemblies.

From Henry's standpoint differences between races became minimal under the experience of love. Yet his sternness led to some anxious moments. One of these occurred in the classroom. He was teaching arithmetic and explaining a problem on the blackboard. To see if his students were paying attention to his explanation, he turned to face the class. He noticed a student sitting in the back of the room playing with a pocketknife. He asked him in a stern tone of voice to put away the knife and pay attention. Henry continued to write. After a brief period, he again turned to the class and again saw the young man using the blade to clean his fingernails. Henry urged him to put away the knife. Once more he went to work at the board. A third time he turned around and saw the young man still playing with the knife. This time Henry walked toward him and, as he approached, the student rose from his desk and with knife open moved toward the rear of the room and into the hallway on the second floor. Henry followed him and spoke gently, "Be a good boy. Give me the knife."

Suddenly he grabbed the boy's arms, wrestled the knife out of his hand, held him by the nape of the neck, and kicked him down the stairs. The next day Henry learned that the boy's mother had come to see President Meibohm and that an investigation was to take place. Henry welcomed it. After the meeting with mother and son, Henry was asked to permit the boy to return to the class. He was more than willing to do that. Without any hesitation or reservation, he told the boy's mother, "If there is any repetition of an incident like this, I refuse to be held responsible for your son's life." That settled the matter. The young man returned. Oddly enough, he became one of the better students during that year.

As there were problem students, there were also students who added to Henry's joy as a teacher. One of them was Albert Dominick, for four years one of the highest achievers at Luther College.

Henry became acquainted with a number of white teachers who taught in the Lutheran parochial schools of the city. In spite of the fact that a white person working among Blacks was not accepted by the white population of New Orleans, including Lutheran Christians, Henry cultivated some lasting friendships. Paul Moerbe, John Schoenhardt, Richard Wismar, Erich Heintzen, Elmer Groth were but a few, and their companionship meant much to Henry.

These friends gathered occasionally for good times in each other's homes. Excellent cuisine spiced with sparkling wines and refreshing beer helped fill the hours with laughter and joy. Again and again they affirmed that teaching young people did not bring riches, but it did have some rewards. Seventy-five dollars a month was Henry's salary during his four years' service. His sons, Eric and John, earned more by selling newspapers, caddying at Lakeview Country Club, hustling popcorn and cokes at Heineman Park, and selling palms and crocheted handkerchiefs made by Helen.

Never idle, Henry's evangelistic spirit prompted him to start a preaching mission in Lakeview, a suburb of the city. The Hasenkampfs, a white couple with six children, opened their home to Henry to conduct divine services and to instruct the young. They also introduced the Naus to the American customs of picnicking, shopping, and auto rides to Audubon and City Parks. When Hope Lutheran Church in the Carrollton area of New Orleans needed help, Henry responded. His spirit of mission and ministry drove him on. His life was fully dedicated to his call: "Go and Tell."

Daily living continued to bring its problems and sorrows. Fights in the streets and at school consumed a great part of the boys' time in the Nau family, especially in the early months after arrival. German immigrants, especially those arriving shortly after World War I, were not welcome in a town of French and Spanish tradition. Numerous times Eric and John felt the piercing thorns high up in palm trees where they were forced to take refuge. The front room of the house was sprayed with watermelon rind and debris of all kinds. Helen had to nurse their black eyes one after another, including one sported by John on his confirmation day.

Adjustment to American customs, school attendance, learning the English language — all had to be faced by the children, with additional problems for Henry and Helen. The parents sent their children to Zion Lutheran School on Claiborne Street in uptown New Orleans. Teacher Paul Moerbe was sympathetic, but the venture ended in failure. John got into a fight. Henry whipped him for it and was happy that the incident coincided with the end of the school year.

Henry worried over the problem of getting his children into school for the fall of 1921. He met an elderly teacher, John Schoenhardt, who taught at St. John's Lutheran School. Schoenhardt came to the rescue by teaching Eric, John, Esther, and Mary Ann enough English so that they could enter their respective grades on time.

A bitter pill had to be swallowed when Helen's brother came to live with them. Walter Hempfing had come to the United States to study for the ministry at Concordia Seminary in St. Louis but had gone astray and had left the seminary. At the request of Helen's father, Henry had agreed to see what he could do with the profligate. For a time he lived a respectable life. He even kept company with a fine young Christian lady, a member of a prominent Lutheran family and a member of St. John's Church. Finally his actions became so reprehensible that Walter was asked to leave. Helen tearfully bade her brother good-bye. Nothing was ever heard of him from that day on. The family was never allowed to mention his name.

Another sorrow for the family was the news that Helen's mother had died. Even though she was not near her parents, she was very close to them and she wished she had seen her mother once more. But she consoled herself with the understanding that God had not included this in His plan for her. In 1923, when the devastating inflation hit Germany, she prevailed on Henry to borrow $25,000.00 to send to Chemnitz to save her father's business. The business still failed and Henry paid back every penny of the debt. The children knew nothing about this, but the austere everyday living conditions reflected the family's financial plight. Yet, Henry and Helen remained tithers for the work of the Lord and were grateful for the many blessings that came their way.

Family sicknesses were rare. Mary Ann suffered from asthma, but the kind and generous services of Dr. Jacob Isaacson, who lived next door, lightened the burden. Henry enjoyed exceptionally good health, a blessing indeed, since he had no life insurance. There were cut feet, black eyes, rusty nails piercing foot and body, which necessitated an occasional trip to Charity Hospital, but all in all, the Nau family was extremely healthy.

New Orleans was a time for Henry to become adjusted to life in America and to the experiences that were to follow. The great interlude had begun, with mixed feelings on his part. How long would it be before he and Helen could return to their first love — India — was anyone's guess.

While Henry worked, walked, worried, wondered, dreamed, planned — all for the mission of God in New Orleans — an anonymous letter dated January 16, 1923, arrived at the Mission Board of the Synodical Conference in St. Louis. It read:

> In conclusion, permit me to say that I think I have succeeded admirably in getting myself hopelessly entangled, and that if you wish to know what I really consider the very best thing to do under the circumstances, my advice is to get someone in my place. Perhaps Dr. Nau would be the man to make superintendent. Let him study the institution with its student body and faculty for a year before you decide whether to go on with building or to

make a change. I have failed, and in the midst of my failure I must distrust my own ability to see things aright and should feel better satisfied if you would not follow any of the plans I mentioned before but decided to put an observer in charge for a year.

The Synodical Conference had been organized in 1878 to carry on work among the Negroes in the Southland. Most of their congregations and preaching missions were located in the eastern part of the United States, from New York to New Orleans. Work had been established in St. Louis, Chicago, St. Paul, Los Angeles, Houston, and other cities. Many elementary schools for Christian education of Negro children had been organized, together with two schools of higher learning — Immanuel Lutheran College in Greensboro, North Carolina, and Alabama Lutheran Academy in Selma, Alabama.

Immanuel College had been founded by a German scholar, Nils J. Bakke, on March 2, 1903, in Concord, North Carolina, where he instructed five boys in the second story of Grace Lutheran School. The organizational motivating force behind him had been the Synodical Conference. By May, 1903, the enrollment had increased to eleven. Coeducation was inaugurated in 1904. The school consisted of two rooms. The larger room served as a classroom by day and as a dormitory for male students by night. The smaller room served as Bakke's quarters. An old dilapidated house in the rear of the church was, by permission of the congregation, transformed into a combination kitchen-dining room. John Philip Smith, the pastor of Grace Lutheran Church, and his teacher, Henry L. Person, rendered valuable assistance by teaching several class periods per week. After two years of existence in Concord, the conference resolved in 1905 to move the institution to Greensboro, the center of Negro work in the Carolinas. 13½ acres of land were purchased on East Market Street. Bakke served as president from 1903 to 1911. Frederick Berg succeeded him from 1911 to 1919 and continued as professor of theology until 1936. Smith, who was a member of the faculty from the time of the institution's founding, served as president from 1919 to 1925. He was the writer of the letter which brought Henry to the attention of the Mission Board of the Synodical Conference.

CHAPTER 10

In the summer of 1925 Henry received a call to Immanuel Lutheran College and accepted it, with the understanding that a girls' dormitory was to be erected immediately. The board gave him no argument, and the family made all preparations to leave New Orleans.

The family spent the last night in the Bethlehem Orphans' Home at St. Peter's Street near the levee of the Mississippi River. It was a never-to-be forgotten night. Swarms of mosquitoes filled the dormitory and pestered every sleeper throughout the night. The next morning Eric and John, who knew something about New Orleans history, told their father that they had relived the Battle of New Orleans.

Henry may also have fought a battle that night, not with insects but with thoughts. Filled with doubts, he placed his future in the hands of God.

The following afternoon the family boarded a train bound for Greensboro, North Carolina, via Mobile, Alabama, and Atlanta, Georgia. Henry and Helen were disturbed and embarrassed at times by their children's behavior in the coach, but after about 28 hours they arrived haggardly tired and happy to be met at the station by William Kampschmidt, a professor at Immanuel. His model-T Ford was a suitable means of transportation to carry the family to his home on the campus, located about a mile and a quarter east of the heart of the city of Greensboro. On arrival, the children saw the table set for the evening meal. Henry and Helen warned their children to hold back and not to give the impression of having been starved for the past month. Their words fell on deaf ears. The potato salad, heaped high on a platter with all the trimmings, disappeared almost instantaneously.

After the first night, spent in the home of the Kampschmidts, Henry lost no time in readying for occupancy the president's home, located at 210 Luther Street, near the Administration Building. It was a large wooden structure of colonial architecture, with certain oddities that defied description. Built prior to World War I, it had been the residence of several presidents of the college. It was a two-story dwelling, with four bedrooms and a bath upstairs, and three rooms with a kitchen downstairs. The exterior was surrounded on three sides by a veranda covered in front of the house, uncovered to the south, and screened to the east. This was to be home for the Nau family from 1925 to 1946. Henry and Helen were quite satisfied with the home despite the lack of both cooling and heating facilities. The children soon called the place "Nau's Rest Haven," after an institution for people with nervous disorders. This public facility was comparatively isolated, and the Naus were within earshot of only two faculty families.

In 1925 Greensboro had 50,000 inhabitants. 10,000 of these were Blacks, who lived in the eastern section. The only whites in this area occupied the three houses on Immanuel's campus.

Mismanagement by whites as well as Blacks had led to deplorable conditions at the school. According to reports, the "moral conditions of the institution were at a low ebb." Even in Lutheran circles the school had a poor reputation. Teachers were too lax in their academic expectations of the students, many of whom failed even to acquire the necessary textbooks within a reasonable time. Proper respect and discipline were at a premium. It was resolved, therefore, that even though such demands might cost a decrease in the number of students, the faculty would insist "not too slowly but surely" upon their being observed.

To achieve the implementation of good resolutions required some diplomacy, a commodity in which Henry had but slight investment. He was always in difficulty, and had developed the reputation of "no team man" because of his insistence on what he believed to be right. He was motivated by a sense of duty, no matter what the impact might be on his personal ambitions. In view of the utter abandonment with which he made friends and acquired enemies, it was even questionable whether he had any personal ambitions.

Immanuel's Administration Building was a monstrosity. A government survey of the original Administration Building of Immanuel Lutheran College described it in the following words: "The building is a two-story granite structure of an inconsistent mixed and wasteful type of architecture. It is heated by stoves. The interior shows bad workmanship, inexperienced planning, and poor material." It had numberless small towers gracing the roof, with an enormous tower in the center. It was a very ornate and picturesque building; but, as stated in the documents of the school systems of North Carolina, a building which was an excellent example of how *not* to build a school. In the basement were the commissary and the boiler room. On the second floor, which was also the ground floor, were the offices of the faculty members, a large hall for devotional services, several classrooms, and a small library. On the second floor were more classrooms, and the third floor housed male students. Most of the third floor was finished on the inside with beaverboard, which was in terrible condition. The Naus referred to the monstrosity as "The castle on the Rhine."

The only other building on the campus housed the girls. Conditions there were so bad that the Health Department of the City of Greensboro had condemned the use of the building. Yet somehow the members of the board and the faculty had received permission to continue its use.

The campus itself made as bad an impression as the buildings. Not a single stretch of pavement graced the place. All the streets were of dirt covered with the ashes that came from the large furnaces which heated the buildings. The driveways leading to the professors' homes and into the garages were all covered with ashes from the same source. There was no blacktopping for the road leading from East Market Street to the entrance of the Administration Building. Even Luther Street was not paved. Such was the picture at Immanuel when Henry went to work. The entire physical plant reflected the spirit with which the work had been done among the black people of the South by the white Lutherans of the Synodical Conference.

After having lived in a shotgun house for four years in New Orleans, Henry's family found their new living quarters most spacious. The grounds offered room to roam, to run, to play, and to have a super garden. A number of poorly constructed and poorly kept outhouses comprised the rest of the president's compound, but the general layout left no doubt as to the allocation of power and material benefits in this area of Lutheranism.

With a large family to feed, Henry utilized much of the grounds of the president's home for a garden. He also had the necessary manpower in four strong boys. Besides this, he had access to an orchard of pear, apple, and peach trees and to a small vineyard. Everyone in the family helped, for Henry's monetary income never exceeded $225.00 per month during his entire presidency. However, the home with all utilities was part of his take. It was, everything considered, a pleasant place to live, especially in the summertime.

Henry assumed full charge of student supervision and did all studying in his office. This kept him away from the family, who felt that he used his home only for eating and sleeping. He never played with the children outdoors or indoors, for he was busy from early morn until late at night. He did make it a practice to eat supper with the family and to conduct evening devotions.

His fellow faculty members were Frederick Berg, professor of theology; William H. Kampschmidt, professor of mathematics and science; Walter H. Beck, professor of languages and history; Frank Lankenau, professor of English; and Miss Margaret J. Turner, professor of home economics. Later came Arnold Pennekamp and William Gehrke. In supervision of men and women students were Captain Samuel A. Reid, a black man, and his wife, who was matron. The Board of Control of the Synodical Conference consisted of Theodore Graebner, chairman; Christopher F. Drewes, director of missions; Theodore W. Eckhart, treasurer; L.A. Wisler, Emanuel F. Albrecht, Otto C. Boecler, John Daniel, Walter A. Hoenecke, John E. Thoen, and Theodore Walther. Most of these men lived in the area of St. Louis, Missouri. A board of directors located more than 1,000 miles from the location of the college created many problems. Many of these men never saw the institution before, during, or after serving as members of the Board.

Throughout his teaching days at Immanuel, Henry could not specialize but had to acquaint himself with a wide scope of subject matter. There was danger that he would become a "jack of all trades and master of none." But he was always well prepared. The range of subjects included Christian doctrine, biblical history, Lutheran confessions, church history, introduction to the New Testament, Lutheran day school, Lutheran Sunday school, rules of interpretation, methodology, catechetics, history of education, school management, and practice of teaching. Of these, Henry prepared seven. He was spreading himself very thin.

At times he ventured into teaching languages, including Greek, Latin, Hebrew, German, and French. On top of all this he counseled, supervised, and did a bit of public relations. He had few moments for himself, but it was his own decision. He had no time for the preparation of professional papers. The sermons he delivered were well constructed and from an interpreter's standpoint sound, but he never wrote them out in full. His voice was not deep or sonorous, but possessed qualities that helped his listeners remain alert and interested. He communicated as well in the pulpit as in the classroom.

The student body during those years ranged from about 90 to 130 students. They came from various parts of the country, but the majority were from the southern states and especially North Carolina. Not all were Lutheran, and some were of no denomination; however, all of them had to take courses in catechism and in religion. The school not only educated men and women for the teaching profession and the ministry, but served as a very important mission tool.

A grievous disappointment to Henry was the recognition that black people were not receiving cooperation from whites of the area. A comparatively new arrival from Germany, he was not prepared for the many layers of racism that blocked communication in the United States. The city of Greensboro itself, home of the college, hardly recognized the existence of the school he headed as president. In the confines of the city limits were two black colleges well known throughout the southeast and northeast: Agricultural-Technical School, known as A and T, supported by the state of North Carolina; and Bennett College, a school for black women, supported by a millionaire white family, the Pfifers of New York. Immanuel was known only to the people who lived in "Bull Pen," the eastern section of the city.

The teachers at Immanuel were similarly ignored. Not only did the white citizenry pay little or no attention to them, but even the pastors and members of the white Lutheran congregations in the Carolinas and Virginia in effect ostracized them. Henry had few white friends outside of the faculty. One was George Mennen, Sr., of Conover, North Carolina, who had been a fellow seminarian and present at Henry's commissioning service as missionary to India. Invitations to speak to white congregations or to white assemblies and groups of any kind to inform them about his work among the Blacks came seldom, if at all, in those early years. Such segregation forced him to move more and more among the Blacks, who became his friends and his everyday associates. It also partially accounted for a defensive attitude in Henry's relation to the Board of Directors and to pastors of white congregations in the southeastern part of the country.

In the summer of 1926 Henry enjoyed a breather when the Mission Board of the Lutheran Church-Missouri Synod asked him to undertake an inspection of Puerto Rico. He was to determine the possibility of opening missions in that territory of the United States. Henry was happily surprised, for he felt that no one knew of his love for "raw" mission work of the type he had cherished in India. He accepted the charge and made the trip, accompanied by Hans Reuter of Birmingham, Alabama. After a number of weeks in Puerto Rico, he had no difficulty whatsoever with the language of the people. His knowledge of Latin and natural ability to acquire a language helped him speak Spanish so well that he communicated with ease. During the visitation he encouraged a young Puerto Rican, Texadore, to come to Immanuel to study theology so that he could return to Puerto Rico as a missionary. Texadore came, but the project in Puerto Rico ultimately failed. Reuter reported that Henry was a wonderful traveling companion. He was impressed also by Henry's ability to relate readily to the people who lived in that part of the world.

In 1927 a momentous event occurred in Henry's life. On June 7 he received his citizenship papers at the Courthouse of Guilford County, North Carolina. This was a moment for which he had waited and prayed. He thought that it would not be long until the missionary board asked him to serve in India. But, as Henry later expressed it, "The Lord had other thoughts and other ways for me. Our thoughts are not God's thoughts. Our ways are not God's ways." As time passed, he adopted a Calvinistic attitude toward life, "God ordains with absolute authority what will be my destiny." With the coming of the Great Depression of 1929 his hope of returning to India seemed utterly shattered. Regardless of what Henry might think of financial statistics, the Lutheran Church-Missouri Synod was in financial trouble, and mission work was expensive. In Greensboro he stayed.

After his return to Immanuel, Henry learned that the well-laid plans he had made with his three brothers, Peter, J. Henry, and Conrad, to bring their father and mother to the United States were to be realized. Having lost all their possessions in the financial depression of Germany in 1923 and penniless by 1926, Peter and Katherine came to Greensboro to begin a new life. They moved into a small house situated on a five-acre plot of land, located between Greensboro and Bessemer City. Henry's son Eric had purchased it from Hans Naether, a former professor at Immanuel, with monies he earned as shipping clerk in an overall factory. Under the expert knowledge and careful manipulation of the land by Peter, the five acres blossomed like the Garden of Eden. The beautiful miniature farm that developed was a joy not only to the aged couple but also to the children of Henry and Helen. Sale of milk, eggs, and other farm products helped make the farm profitable. The Naus purchased all their milk from the small dairy operated by Peter and Katherine. All in all, a pleasant relationship developed between father, mother, son, and family. For the first time in 25 years, Henry was able to spend time with his parents.

CHAPTER 11

Henry's life as head administrator of Immanuel Lutheran was a story of trouble heaped on trouble. Despite the efforts of *The Pioneer,* a Negro church publication, which advocated a four-year college for Greensboro, the Synodical Conference, meeting at Quincy, Illinois, in 1930, resolved to add only two years. Although the high school had been accredited by the State of North Carolina in 1923, this two-year program failed to receive recognition from the Southern Association of Colleges and Secondary Schools. This state of affairs was especially hard on Immanuel's students who had come from the state of Alabama to prepare for teaching in the black schools back home, only to discover upon graduation that Alabama would not issue them a teaching license.

Faced with the perilous weakness in his institution, Henry worked untiringly for the accreditation of the junior college. It was a herculean struggle, but he finally secured accreditation not only from Alabama but other states in which Immanuel's graduates were to teach. This achievement greatly furthered the cause of young Blacks in the South.

The problem of accreditation of the junior college was somehow connected with a more serious one that attacked the very life of the institution. It was the never-to-go-away problem of the "open-door" versus the "closed-door" policy. Open-door meant that any prospective student, Lutheran or non-Lutheran, could be considered for admission. Closed-door meant that only members of Lutheran churches could be accepted at Immanuel. When Henry arrived at Immanuel, the open-door policy was in effect, and Henry was convinced that it was the only approach consistent with Immanuel's avowed mission thrust.

After Henry's arrival the members of the Synodical Conference became more and more embroiled in doctrinal concerns. High on the agenda was the question of "Unionism." Put simply, this meant: "Can a Lutheran of the Synodical Conference pray and worship with members of other Lutheran groups, not to speak of non-Lutheran denominations, such as Baptists, Methodists, etc.?" Immanuel had not only been debilitated under a financial crunch, but it was now caught in the crossfire of theologians' debate. The situation called for toughness of character.

The more Henry became involved in the problem the more he realized that doctrinal concerns over the open-door policy seemed to be in direct proportion to the financial stress experienced by the supporting church bodies. He also observed that the deeply entrenched chauvinism of the proponents for the closed-door policy became more verbal whenever a worker in the field who had been educated at Immanuel did not perform his duties as expected by the members of the board or a superintendent in the field.

Henry knew the arguments well. One member of Immanuel's board asked:
Why add the leaven of sectarianism . . . by enrolling armies not of our faith (sic!) simply to swell the number? . . . We need workers with as much Lutheran background and training as possible, not such who come to us for a cheap education and then, because they haven't enough money to go

elsewhere, . . . drift into our Theological Department with the result only too often that we get hastily made over, half-baked candidates for the ministry, of doubtful value to us.

In an even more bitter vein a worker in the mission field wrote: "The training of our few Negro workers during the past twenty-five years has cost our church an unjustifiable sum of money. The same number could have been trained and better trained at a small sum if we had restricted ourselves to Lutheran boys only." He then went on to complain about a graduate of non-Lutheran background who "had to be criticized for neglectful work and left us and became a Methodist preacher." Of another he said, "We find his doctrinal position and fixed religious views are not what they should be." Others took what appeared to be on the surface a road of genuine principle by suggesting that Immanuel could even lay itself open to a charge of proselytizing.

Henry met all these biased non-sequiturs and racist judgments. On March 30, 1938 he wrote:

> Many of these arguments present a straw man. Most of the sectarian students coming to us are sent by their parents or guardians because they have been attracted by the religious training given in the school. The parents want the kind of religious training we are giving for their children. Others enter fully knowing that ours is a religious school. . . . Everyone is asked to attend the religious lessons, Sunday School, and divine services. They know this rule of our school when entering. Their attention is especially called to this feature. They are at liberty to say, "We do not want the religious instruction" and to enter another school according to their liking. Those who enter cheerfully with a full knowledge of the practice of the school can surely not be said to have been compelled to attend religious exercises. Anyone who calls this proselytizing or compelling should once more return to the seminary for one year more of study to learn what these terms mean.

The fighter continued:

> It is a dishonest insinuation to create the opinion in the mind of the reader that we are here only concerned about the secular education approved by a government office. Our aim is, indeed has always been, and, God willing, will forever be, the molding of truly Christian character. I could even express this aim in words more adequately than by this much-used and very-little-understood word, character, and also [by reference to] the preparation of the students for efficient work in our schools and churches; and [I would like to emphasize the aim] which was not overlooked at the time of the foundation of the school but is now, sad to say, very frequently and, as it seems, very conveniently forgotten — to serve as a missionary agency in the case of those who of their own free will have placed themselves under our care, although they do not as yet belong to our church.

He stormed on in equally agitated syntax:

> The school has never solicited students for funds. . . . The school has, in years gone by, advertised itself as a school which had a good thing to give eveyone who wanted it. If that is called soliciting, call it that way. It is not wrong. Call it proselytizing if you want. It is not wrong. If that kind of advertising soliciting is wrong, the *Lutheran Hour,* too, is wrong. The

Lutheran Hour solicits funds. As long as I am president of Immanuel Lutheran College this kind of soliciting or proselytizing, if you prefer to call it so, will always be done. I shall tell privately, publicly, whenever and whatsoever place I get a chance, of the good thing we have here. If anyone wants to stop that, he may try. He will have to remove me from the presidency of Immanuel Lutheran College if that is to be stopped. I deny, however, emphatically that by training sectarian students in the pure word of God we help building [sic] up the sectarian churches. The sectarian churches as sectarian churches exist by, instead of, their false teaching. We teach the pure word of God. The pure word of God never builds a sectarian church. It counteracts and the mind destroys that which makes these churches sectarian churches; namely, false teaching. What the word of God builds in these churches is the unsanctioned word of God [that is, the truth of the Bible finds expression despite an otherwise erroneous position, Ed.] concerning which we confess, and I think confess with some appreciation, that it is also to be found in the erring churches.

As the controversy raged and brought charges and countercharges, he retorted:

Why am I a Lutheran after all? Because in the Lutheran Church I can best work out my salvation with fear and trembling, and because in the Lutheran Church I can best help building the only holy Church of the third article of the apostle's creed which alone has the promise that the gates of hell shall not prevail against her. And this I can do best in the Lutheran Church because it has the pure word of God and the sacraments as instituted by Christ.

With such rhetoric, Henry urged that it was best to continue the open-door policy as it had been practiced at the school since its founding and to stop rehashing the same useless matter before every convention of the Synodical Conference.

Rather than refuse any prospective student because of religious affiliation, Henry was ready to lay his job on the line. For a quarter of a century of service to his church as president of Immanuel Lutheran College he fought a battle that cost him much in physical, emotional, and spiritual resources. He recognized the reality of hard times and was well aware that financial economy and responsibility had to be practiced. The average cost for the operation of the educational institution from 1929 to 1942, a period of 13 years, amounted to about $13,396 per year. This did not include monies received from the students for tuition, board, and some incidentals. While this was a modest sum of money for the operation of a school with about 90 to 100 students, many individuals who favored the closed-door policy called attention to the fact that over a two-year period it cost the Synodical Conference $6,000 per year for the training and equipping of a theological graduate. Such an expenditure was held far in excess of anything paid at any other institution of the church. Whenever such a comparison in finances was made, Henry felt deep down in his marrow that it was always connected with the one underlying target, the open-door policy, which permitted non-synodical conference members to enroll at the school.

Appalled by the prospect of church bodies prepared to sacrifice the mission of God at the altar of fiscal expediency, he proved by actual figures that, considering the salaries of faculty members, Immanuel was by no means a great expense to the church. Henry's salary at that time amounted to $195 per month and the use of a house with utilities. In the lush years from 1944 to 1946, salaries of faculty and staff were so low that it was difficult to secure competent people. In 1947 the Mission Board agreed to raise Henry's salary by ten dollars a month and other faculty members by five dollars a month. On receiving this information, Henry replied to the executive director of the Board:

> I have not the courage to disclose this magnanimity of the Board to the teachers who shall receive a five-dollar raise. Kindly relieve me of the humiliation to make this known to them. Please write a personal letter to them. I shall say nothing. At the same time, I ask you to inform the Board that I shall not accept the ten-dollar raise as long as my fellow workers receive a five-dollar raise. I reserve, however, the right for myself to go out into the city of Greensboro and earn on the sideline [he did not know the word "moonlighting"] as much money as I need in addition to the salary which I draw in order to make ends meet.

The man who once challenged a fellow student to a sabre match was at it again.

In the midst of all of these arguments and problems, Henry realized that there was one almost insoluble situation. Immanuel did not graduate enough theological students, that is, young men who served as ministers among the Blacks. The conditions for this existing scarcity were such that he was handcuffed in solving it. The low salaries paid to black ministers, the paternalistic spirit of the white superintendents in the field, the general relationship between the workers in the field and the members of an all-white and absentee mission board, and the general attitude of white workers toward black workers contributed to the school's inability to attract the desired number of ministerial students.

As early as the 1930's Nau pleaded for all black students desiring to study for the ministry to be educated at Springfield, Illinois, where the Missouri Synod had its practical seminary for white students. Besides treating the black student as an equal this plan would have eliminated the Theological Department of Immanuel and saved money. The administration of that seminary, headed by Henry B. Hemmeter, strongly opposed this recommendation. Henry's relation to the black man was born of the gospel; theirs was dictated by the social and economic status quo. Years ahead of his time, not only in the area of race relations, but in others that related to evangelism at home and abroad, he was mission inspired. Serving people with the gospel was his primary objective.

Instead of disappearing, the financial problem grew more acute. By 1946 Immanuel had hired a number of black teachers. A black instructor received a monthly salary of $130. Henry urged that the pay scale be raised to $175. He informed the Board that this amount was in keeping with the salaries paid to teachers in the area of North Carolina, South Carolina, and Virginia. He called attention to the fact that two of his teachers had received offers from schools in the eastern part of the state of North Carolina with a guarantee of one third more salary than they received at Immanuel.

Nau's interest in raising salaries extended to every worker in the mission field. The low salaries of the workers forced their wives to find work. Such economic recourse was contrary to the policy of the governing body, and many young pastors and teachers found themselves in difficulty with the superintendent of the field. But when the salaries were not forthcoming, Henry encouraged the young men to have their wives work in spite of the existing rule.

Henry lived by the principle that every person, regardless of color or station, was worthy of his hire. A black man paid just as much for his groceries as he; had just as many bills. He could scarcely contain himself, therefore, when in the early forties the Missouri Synod accumulated a surplus of $360,000 and added the sum to its contingent fund. The Missouri Synod's hierarchy was euphoric in its plaudits. Henry, knowing of the pitifully small salaries paid to many workers in the mission field where blacks were in the majority, let loose a storm of indignation straight from the Old Testament prophet Jeremiah. "Woe unto him . . . that useth his neighbor's service without wages, and giveth him not for his work." He made no reference to the wages of the white workers, especially not to his own. He felt that the white workers did not suffer want. But since the Lutheran Church-Missouri Synod had a surplus, and since the Mission Board knowingly permitted low salaries among black workers to exist, he did not believe that the Lord's blessing would rest on the Synod or the Synodical Conference in their work. He suggested that the Missouri Synod immediately call for the salary list of all black workers, review their salaries and then use a part of the surplus to remove the stigma mentioned in Jeremiah.

Henry's request came to the attention of Dr. John W. Behnken, president of the Missouri Synod. Behnken sent the notice of Henry's remarks to Louis A. Wisler. Wisler replied to the president that he saw no good reason why the scrapping doctor in North Carolina should multiply the president's worries. He called the suggestion an untimely explosion, and noted that a committee of the Synodical Conference was at the time doing a thorough study of the salary question in the Negro mission.

Low salaries for black workers remained a reality and eventually spelled trouble. In 1942 a black minister in the Carolina field, Colbert J. Malloy, tendered his resignation with deep emotion and reluctance and "with malice toward none." The resignation was to take effect on January 10, 1943. In support of his resignation he said that his ministry had not been appreciated and supported; that he had not received a fair living salary; and that a sizeable portion of his promised salary had been denied him, while entreaties for a satisfactory adjustment had been met with stony silence or excited humor, which attempted to minimize the problem.

The case of Harry Haysbert involved the principle of ministers' wives working to assist in maintaining a decent standard of living. Haysbert's wife found gainful employment. The board urged her to quit work. Unwilling to comply, Haysbert resigned from his pastorate at St. Mark's Lutheran Church in June, 1942. He took the action without any ill will toward the Mission Board or the local congregation. He felt that "it was a sudden decision, but time and tide wait for no man."

When such problems reached Henry's attention, his heart was troubled, and he lost no time writing to the Mission Board to express his feeling. His words went off well honed. He accused the board of inability to inspire him and the workers in the field to do their best. They replied with a reprimand to the effect that his words were a planned and studied blast at the board, another monkey wrench thrown into the cogwheels to rule out cheerful cooperation. Far from granting the fact that they themselves were uninspiring, the board threw the charge back into Henry's teeth and ordered the president of Immanuel and his colleagues to inspire the workers to do their best. Stung by the insensitivity of the church's bureaucracy, the embattled petrel, in one of his darkest moments, wrote to his son John about the advisability of taking a call to a congregation. His son answered, "Papa, you would not last thirty days serving a white congregation in the Missouri Synod." The common worker in the Lord's vineyard respected and loved Henry, but to his superiors he was an enigma.

Strangely enough, Henry was more often ready to keep the peace than to kindle the fires of controversy. After many stormy meetings he expressed his willingness to return to his work and with sincere efforts to reestablish confidence, to remove prejudices, and to develop a spirit of cooperation. He even acquiesced in the heated discussions over salaries by rendering the assurance, "I shall follow your advice." He wrote letters thanking the members of the board for their kind consideration of the problem pertaining to the school and its operation. In the spring of 1945 he seemed to have buried the hatchet. In typical Nau phrasing he wrote: "Finally I wish to thank you for the warm tone of your letter. Confidence begets confidence, and a warm stove makes everybody feel warm and happy."

Henry's attitude toward finances and salaries did not foster friendly relations with the board members. Nor did the appearance of a written review of the mission field by John T. Mueller, who included Immanuel in his survey, improve their strained relationship. Many persons received a copy, but not Henry. He saw a copy sent by Andrew Schulze of St. Louis to Clemonce Sabourin, a friend and former student. Angered that he had not received a copy from Mueller, he wrote him for one. He was furious when told that he would have to wait for the board to send him one. Henry's reply expressed his sorrow that "we are not thought reliable or trustworthy enough to be favored with a similar copy."

Such mistrust, such wrangling, such difference of opinion forced him to place all in perspective as he exclaimed, "Give us the $100,000 and we will spend it and then tell you what we did with it!" The outcry showed that Henry believed, as he had in India, that men in mission both in the United States as well as elsewhere should make their own decisions and then make their reports to the controlling body. He strongly believed that the proper decisions for his work could not be made by men who called the shots sitting far away from the field of operation. It was this condition, he felt, which was responsible for the mistrust in school policies governing admissions, finances, the hiring of teachers, and also the review of the work of the institution and its relation to the rest of the work among black people.

CHAPTER 12

Among complaints made by the governing board of Immanuel College was the charge that the moral life of the students was not the best. Henry well knew that his own church's all-white preparatory schools were no incubators for holiness and he recognized the diversionary tactic as part of a larger attack on the open-door policy. He tried to make his reaction as printable as possible:

> . . . the presence of non-Lutherans does not detract from the confessional-
> ism of the institution. There is more religious teaching here than at our other
> institutions. Religion is not optional but every student takes the prescribed
> course. There is one hour of religion every day. There is chapel every
> afternoon, quite religious too, and also evening prayer. Every boarding
> student attends church twice on Sunday at our Lutheran church. All stu-
> dents are under the moral obligations to read the word of God, to learn it,
> and to live by it.

Henry's protective response was part of his conviction that he enjoyed a unique rapport with his students, and it was questionable whether any other white man in similar circumstances could have done what he did.

In general Henry was pleased with the deportment of his students. Minor infringement of the rules of the institution took place, but the transgressors received Christian discipline. Over a seven-year period in the thirties the faculty had not suspended a single student for misbehavior.

During Henry's tenure the school had inaugurated a system of demerits. After accruing a number of demerits, a student, whether boy or girl, was obliged to do chores without pay to lessen his demerits. Henry often supervised these chores, particularly those done by the boys. The girls were supervised by the dormitory mother. Other tasks done by students received a nominal remuneration, and one of Henry's greatest pleasures was the discovery of opportunities for young people to earn money, especially in the summer months. Students painted buildings, repaired furniture, scrubbed rooms, and manicured the campus — all supervised by Henry. He demanded a good day's work for a good day's pay, even though the going hourly rate was 25 cents. Whenever he found someone loafing, he threatened, "The ducks will get your money." By that he meant that he would deduct some from their salary at the end of the week. Despite the "forced" labor and Henry's demand for discipline, the students felt comfortable with their president. His compassionate understanding endeared him to them.

Occasionally Henry had to lower the boom. One such case involved a student known as Fab. Fab was a good trumpet player, but he was also preparing for the ministry. He loved to blow the instrument and regarded his ability as a God-given talent to be used not only for entertainment of the students at the school, but in play for pay. He contracted to work in an orchestra at Jonesboro Park, not far from the campus. At this amusement area, a public dance pavilion was the center of attraction and Fab was the outstanding member of the dance band. Henry felt that Fab should not blow his trumpet in such a setting. It was unbecoming a ministerial student. Besides that, Fab returned in the early hours of the morning and caught up on his sleep by missing classes. Henry confronted

Fab with the problem and strongly urged him to stop his trumpet playing at Jonesboro Park. The trumpet, he said, had to make way for study and full application to his work at the school. Fab smiled, listened to the admonition, but did not heed it. He continued to play and at the same time felt he could outfox old "Doc."

Henry learned of Fab's double dealing and decided to do something about it. At once Henry became the hunter and Fab the hunted. So it was that one night Henry waited and waited. The clock struck three. Henry stayed in his office, the minutes ticking away one by one. About daybreak he went into the hallway to get a better view of the rear door to the Administration Building through which Fab had to pass to get to his bedroom on the second floor. Suddenly a dark figure appeared in the doorway. Henry knew it was Fab. At the same time Fab saw the threatening figure in the hallway. He knew he could not pass without being recognized and tried to outfox the hunter. He quickly disappeared to his left into the open area that led to the basement; but instead of running down into the basement, he hid behind the door. Henry, quick of foot, ran into the area leading into the basement and sensed immediately that Fab was hiding behind the door. Without warning, he rammed his 210 pounds with a mighty thrust against the door and squeezed Fab's 140 pounds between the door and the wall of the building. Fab the hunted was at the mercy of the hunter. Henry confronted Fab with the information that his horn-blowing days as a student were at an end. He ordered him to go upstairs, pack his belongings, and leave the institution as quickly as possible. This was Henry, the disciplinarian.

In other circumstances Henry was most sympathetic to anyone who had a problem and needed his love and assistance. The girls of the school were like his own children. He was well aware of the fact that they were black and he was white, but he had transcended the color line. Frequently they benefited from his wise counsel. They heard him say, "No one eats the soup as hot as it is boiled." He walked the campus with his arms around the shoulders of the students, both male and female. They looked to him as their friend, as their confessor, and as a father figure. Even though he was criticized by some members of the faculty for his relationships with the students, particularly the female students, he never flinched but continued to express his concern for them in his own manner. This was Henry, the compassionate, at times projecting total insensitivity, yet hearty and filled with warmth.

Ordinarily Henry practiced merciful diplomacy with the students, but when the conduct of students, despite all remonstrance, did not come up to his expectation, he would deal directly with them. If a student obtained illegal whiskey, better known as "white lightning," and made a public display of himself after imbibing too much, he heard "Doc" read the riot act. On one occasion, after a weekend party held in Reid Hall, the girls' dormitory, a student was so deeply under the influence of white lightning that he frightened the wits out of one of the party goers. Henry, who was in the vicinity, was informed of the condition of the student and lost no time finding him. He also wasted no time informing the inebriated young man that he was no longer a member of the student body.

As friend and counselor, as teacher and supervisor, he formed close ties with students that lasted beyond graduation. Among them were Robert Ingram,

Lloyd Gauthreaux, James Justice, Frank Thompson, Arthur Chambers, Harrington Rivers, William Eddleman, Felton Vorice, Wilbur Twitty, Albert Dominick, Raymond Neely, Clemonce Sabourin, George Williston, Carter Winbush, Harry Haysbert, Osborn Smallwood, Henry Sorrell, Joseph Lavalais, and others. As years passed there were Moses Dickinson, Samuel Gailes, Lionel Sabourin, Herbert McClean, Edward Bodley, Charles Graeber, John Calhoun, Howard Ford, Othneil Thompson, Robert King, Paul Leacraft, and William Hartsfield. These were only a few whom Henry regarded as his responsibility and to whom he gave his friendship. He also included Haskew Bates, Harvey Lehman, DeWitt Robinson, Luther Robinson, Henry Grigsby, Peter Hunt, Winston Pledger, Otis Demouy, Walter Hart, Eddie Forney, Hayes Skinner, Lester Charles, Rockfeller Jenkins, and Theodore Johnson.

Through the years the circle of students and friends grew to include a Harry Demouy, a Philip Samuel, a Lucius Means, a Brice Thompson, an Elson Demouy, a Harvey Robinson, a John Jenkins, a John Skinner, and a William Graeber. All of these were men preparing for the ministry and therefore had a special place in the heart and life of Henry. Yet he also had a deep interest for the girl students. Among them were Maggie and Gertrude Holley from Greensboro, North Carolina, whose father and mother meant a great deal not only to Henry but to the entire Nau family. Many other individuals whose names appeared on the student roster during Henry's presidency became his lasting friends and the beneficiaries of his concern and care. He ignored no one.

Henry's moral philosophy permeated the life of his students. In those days there was no apology made for imposing a white German-oriented ethic or system of mores on the student body of another culture. Black Lutherans would have considered this an incentive for sending their children to Greensboro. Punctuality and regularity in attendance of classes was mandatory. Tardiness was equivalent to laziness. Extravagant finery was tabu, even at commencement exercises. Good behavior, Christian piety, and faithful application were considered the best ornaments for all students. Regulations for the boarding students stated that no boarding student was allowed to leave the city under any circumstances without the president's permission. They were not to make debts without the permission of the president. All students received "duty work." They were to keep themselves clean, as well as their rooms, beds, clothing, and the buildings they occupied. Students who had the written consent of their parents, or who were 18 years of age or over, could smoke in restricted areas.

The tobacco regulation especially bore the impress of Henry's feeling about the use of this weed. He began smoking at the age of 13 and had no objection to his boys smoking, if only they informed him when they wanted to start. His sons, Eric and John, decided in their early teens to smoke some corn silk wrapped in newspaper. They hid behind the barn, but Esther saw them and reported their mischief to Henry. Henry ordered Esther to call the boys; he wanted to speak to them. When the boys came, he said, "I was thirteen years old when I started to smoke. I have no objection to you smoking, but I don't want you to do it behind my back."

Henry was a pipe smoker, nothing fancy, just a simple corncob pipe. This he seldom discarded unless it burnt through or someone gave him a new one as a present. Through the years he received many excellent pipes as gifts. These graced the desk in his home, but he always smoked the corncob filled with Granger tobacco. His children presented him with five-pound cans of the stuff as birthday and Christmas presents. At such times he broke out in a smile and expressed his thanks for what he regarded as a most gracious gift. In 1935, after having smoked for 42 years, he noticed a "palpitation of the heart." Believing that smoking was the cause, he stopped and never touched tobacco again. His doctor was greatly surprised that he did not have a bad reaction since Henry had smoked for so many years and his body had adjusted to the nicotine, but he had no ill effects whatsoever. The only ill effect, if one were to call it that, was the bewilderment of the children of the faculty families. They would go home and tell their mothers that "Doc" without his corncob pipe was not Dr. Nau. He had used the pipe so long that the molars on his left side showed perfect indentations where the pipe stem fit.

Henry could be gruff and crusty in his dealing with students, faculty, and members of the board, and he faced many problems head on, but he harbored no continuing bitterness against his fellow man. Rather than jeopardize the mission of God, he would apologize for his words and actions if the occasion demanded it. Despite his cry in Philadelphia, "We cannot get justice," he remained committed to his mission of teaching and living the gospel.

He harbored some mistrust in his working with individual members of the board and certain workers in the mission field but nursed no malice. During the days of the heated open-door versus closed-door policy debate, the board, without Henry's knowledge, asked William Gehrke to evaluate the conditions at Immanuel. Gehrke balked at the request:

> I wish to be excused from replying to your questionnaire regarding Immanuel Lutheran College. Instead I would suggest that these questions be submitted to the faculty; particularly, since they deal not with the closing of the institution but with the existing situation. Kindly picture to yourself the position in which I find myself if I, while serving in the classrooms, secretly review the institution.

When Henry learned of this clandestine effort to get information, he knew that his mistrust of certain individuals was not an outbreak of paranoia.

Whether Henry regarded Gehrke as a stool pigeon of the board or not remained a mystery. Yet Henry's every activity was carefully monitored and relayed to the members of the board. One such report arrived after a non-Lutheran student of Immanuel accidentally drowned in a local lake and was buried at a church service held in a Methodist church. Henry considered it proper that as president of the school he pay his respects at the funeral service of one of his students. He entered the church and took a seat in the very last pew. He chose this place purposely so that no one would notice him either from the pulpit or from the altar. He had a premonition that the Methodist minister would, on recognition, call on him to say a few words. He was also well aware of what many board members and a certain member of his faculty might think concerning the practice of "unionism." Unionism included the act of praying with non-Lutherans. Aware of his church's stricture, Henry tried to be as inconspicuous as possible.

The minister delivered a brief oration. After he finished speaking, he looked over the congregation and noticed a white face in the midst of all the black ones. Immediately he announced to the congregation that the president of Immanuel Lutheran College was in the audience. He then asked Henry whether, as president of the school attended by the deceased, he would be willing to close the service with a prayer. Henry was in a quandary. Would God be pleased if he passed up an opportunity to speak a word about his faith? Would his church be offended if he accepted the opportunity? Henry was more concerned about what God would think and walked to the front of the congregation. Besides, he felt, the minister could have been more explicit in his statement of the gospel. Therefore, instead of just speaking a prayer he addressed the mourners with a biblical word of comfort anchored in the life and death and resurrection of Jesus Christ. He was convinced that God's Spirit inspired him to make these remarks and that failure to witness to his personal faith would have been a flagrant act of disobedience to the command of his Lord and Master, "Go and preach the gospel to every creature."

This incident produced repercussions beyond his wildest expectations. The news spread far and wide that he had attended the funeral and had spoken to the audience. Unknown to Henry, one of his fellow faculty members wrote a letter to St. Louis giving all details. Shortly thereafter Henry received word to attend a board meeting. He was perplexed. Why should he be summoned to a board meeting in St. Louis? What had he done, or what information would he receive at headquarters that would necessitate such a long trip? However, since the order had come, and since he had often attended board meetings, he went to St. Louis. According to his usual practice, he obtained a room at the American Annex and on the next morning went to Concordia Publishing House on South Jefferson Avenue, where the meeting was held.

Henry greeted his friends. The chairman called the meeting to order. A brief devotion followed. Within a short time Henry learned, to his consternation, why he had been called. He was charged with the practice of unionism, which, the board informed him, was conduct unbecoming the president of a Lutheran seminary. Despite the legalism that was in Henry's own nature, he was so overcome by the accusation that for a moment he was at a loss for words. This was most unusual for one who was ordinarily able to express himself rather forthrightly regardless of the situation. When the first shock subsided, he spoke his personal conviction. Looking each member in the eyeball, he expressed the feeling that if they had ordered him to St. Louis to answer the charge of unionism for attending the funeral of a man who had been a student at Immanuel College, an occasion that had given him an opportunity to witness to the saving grace of God, he would immediately leave the gathering and return to Greensboro. Henry sensed the tension. Without a moment's hesitation, he left the room. He strode through the main entrance of the publishing house, walked to the street, and headed for the corner to catch a streetcar to the American Annex. There he intended to gather his few belongings and take the train home. His conscience had frequently bothered him after some of the actions he had taken and words that he had spoken, also to members of the board, but this time he had no scruples whatsoever. He was certain that God approved of what he had done.

He did not know what transpired in the meeting of the board after his departure, but suddenly, John T. Mueller, a personal friend of Henry's since seminary days and a member of the board, approached him as he waited for the streetcar. The board had sent Mueller to urge Henry to rethink his action and to return to the meeting. Henry told Mueller he would return if the members would drop the matter and never refer to it again. Mueller gave him that assurance, and Henry returned. Not a single reference was made again to the incident during the day, but the episode convinced Henry that some of the men of the board had a different spirit than his. His spirit, tempered by work in India, by experiences in the German army, by work among the Blacks in New Orleans and the Carolinas was one of love, openness, and willingness to share his faith. He knew that his understanding of the gospel was in conflict with the interpretation others had expressed in their approach to the problems that surfaced at Immanuel College during his incumbency as president.

Why was he in disagreement with men who appeared to have the same interest at heart, the proclamation of the kingdom of God and the achievement of excellence at Immanuel? Louis A. Wisler, a member of the board, displayed the depths of racism in his own soul when he wrote:

> One distinctive feature of race is its divisiveness. In this respect it may be compared with the confusion of tongues at Babel. Reform endeavor, including the abolition of race distinction under the guise of Christian missionary work, can only result in the greatest harm and obstruction in the kingdom of Christ — the Christian church.

The same man presented these thoughts in a conference essay:

> Had it been His purpose to abolish difference in society, Jesus might have demonstrated it by entering into the house of the Gentiles and eating with them; but there is no evidence that He ever did so. Observance of the race rules and customs concerning segregation in a marriage, in the dining, and in the race association in general and church union in particular is, like the observance of innocent customs, also a matter of Christian liberties subject to the law of charity and wisdom. There is no absolute scriptural necessity for common worship and no necessity at all beyond that of expedience for racial groups to worship in the same building as one congregation. Our business is to preach the gospel, untrammeled by human demands of any kind, and to leave the results to God as it becomes faithful ministers and stewards of the mysteries of God.

Henry had difficulty believing that a conference of Lutheran clergymen could receive such an essay and even offer a vote of thanks to the essayist. Henry's Bible told him that in the kingdom of God there was to be no discrimination based on color, blood, or ethnic grouping. God, as the Father of all, was himself unprejudiced. He did not eliminate distinctions of color, but he showed no preference of white over black or black over white. Henry tried to live by such principle and to persuade everyone to live by it also. He worshiped regularly in black congregations. He felt at home with black people and not only associated with them but tried, to the best of his ability, to understand them. Some Blacks who knew him well said that "he was a white man who could think black." Blacks trusted him, and Henry sincerely tried to prove worthy of that trust.

Since he lived with Blacks, Henry understood their life and problems. In the days of "Jim Crow," he encouraged students to obey the law of the land even though he held the law to be unjust. At the same time he urged Blacks not to allow their humanity to be degraded. "Stand up for your rights!" was his watchword. He invited Blacks to his home and accepted housing with them during the conferences. They were his brothers and sisters in Christ. He reflected very few of the racial feelings that were prevalent in America at that time, especially among American Lutherans. Paradoxical as it may appear, and years before the cry "black is beautiful" became popular, he believed that a Negro should be proud of his race and blackness. Whites resented his stand on race, found him difficult to live with, and mistrusted him, but Henry took it in stride.

Henry had a deep appreciation for the rich ceremonial heritage of blacks and the expressiveness of their worship. In the early days at Immanuel, he attended an important meeting of black educators in Durham, North Carolina. Eric and John accompanied him. It was a 55-mile drive in the model-T Ford. The trip took almost three hours, for Henry regarded 30 miles an hour as flying. The boys tried to encourage their father to drive faster. Whenever a car passed they shouted, "An ice wagon just passed us!" The plea had no effect. The convention opened with a brief service in which the assembled teachers sang "The Old-Time Religion." Eric and John, never having heard the singing of this hymn and not accustomed to the swaying and rhythmic movement of the singers, broke into a nonstop giggle. Henry reprimanded them several times, but the giggling went on. On the way home, Henry gave the boys a lecture. He conveyed in no uncertain terms that he expected them to be respectful of other people's religious practices. They were never to ridicule, but to appreciate.

Holy Rollers worshiped near the campus. The children went to the rustic building to observe their services. Henry gave them permission, but instructed them never to demean the Rollers' worship and their manner of expressing feeling in joyful outbursts of "hallelujahs" and "amens." Even the Rollers' physical expressions and gyrations of rolling and shouting, of dancing, jumping, and shaking were to be respected.

Although many white people in Greensboro thought well of Henry, it was the average inhabitant of "Bull Pen" who appreciated him most. He had the remarkable elasticity to relate to the highest and the lowest, the literate and the illiterate, the moral and the immoral, the righteous and the sinner. Whenever the police department had a problem with someone associated with Immanuel or with anyone else living in the proximity of the campus, it sought advice from Henry. The faculty and students of the two Negro institutions, A & T and Bennett, had the highest respect for him and loved him for his devotion, his dedication, and his consideration. Also white men and women of institutions of higher learning in the area of the North Carolina Piedmont — and there were a number of them — had similar high regard and respect for him. The enigma of his life was that he had difficulties with brothers of his own church, Lutherans of the Missouri Synod and associates in the Synodical Conference.

For a number of years Henry had the dream of creating a regional committee. Such a group could link the interest of the Missionary Board of the Synodical Conference with those of the faculty and student body of Immanuel. Being close to the action, such a group, he thought, could alleviate many problems that were caused simply by poor communication.

In 1947 a part of the dream became reality. The impetus for regional policy-making came not only from Henry's efforts, but also from the freshly organized Southeastern District of the Lutheran Church-Missouri Synod, a district covering geographically the states along the Atlantic Ocean from Maryland to and including Georgia.

After the organization of the district, Henry was drawn into its work by meeting the white workers in white congregations, which brought his work among Blacks to their attention. These contacts were on an individual and a collective basis as he attended conferences and conventions of the district. Gradually, as time passed, he vividly demonstrated his love for the many colleagues serving white congregations. They in turn expressed their appreciation and love for the man who for such a long time had battled almost single-handedly for recognition by his church of Black Lutherans in the Southeast.

In time this work became the responsibility of the Missouri Synod's district in that geographical area and led to the formation of a local board for the institution. The first members of this board were ministers and laymen, all well known to Henry. He especially enjoyed his work with Gustav E. Hageman, Richard P. Meibohm, Otto I. cht, Moses S. Dickinson (a graduate of Immanuel Lutheran College during the days of Henry's administration as president), and William O. Hill. These men contributed to the development of a better relationship between the faculty of the school and the ecclesiastical boards which were responsible to their constituency for the operation of the institution. This is not to say that Henry had found a panacea or had now entered into a bureaucratic utopia. Even with members of the regional board, particularly its chairman, Henry at times had differences of opinion that caused some furor, but the isolation of the twenties and thirties was replaced by the brighter, cooperative days of the forties and early fifties.

CHAPTER 13

Thanksgiving brought a break in academic routines. This national observance spelled slaughter for Henry, and he tackled the task with as much enthusiasm as he had during his youth in Beltershausen. He built a smokehouse to cure ham, blood and liver sausages, and he preserved loins of pork in salt brine. With the help of her husband's butchering expertise Helen was now able to set one of the most delectable tables in town. Also, the sight of Henry straddling a stunned hog to catch its blood and hang it from a crosstie ready for dressing was one of a number of experiences that helped his children develop a more balanced picture of their father, who so often appeared to be overly preoccupied with the work and problems of his school.

Those who knew Henry well were aware that his conversation always centered on his work, especially if it had anything to do with mission. He rarely talked about his family, yet he did manage to project a fatherly image to his children. In the fall of 1926 son Walter entered Concordia Seminary in St. Louis. Eric quit school after his freshman year at Greensboro High to work at the Bluebell Overall Factory. John was scheduled to attend Concordia College, a Lutheran ministerial preparatory school in Conover, North Carolina, a town of 2,000 inhabitants, situated in the foothills of the Appalachian Mountain range. Henry and Helen were unacquainted with the school there and decided to take John by car.

Henry had his model-T Ford readied for the trip, and in high spirits on an early September morning he took the wheel. Helen and John got in, and Eric and Esther went along for the ride — a distance of 100 miles, 30 miles of blacktop and 70 miles of dirt. Service stations were very scarce, so self-service gear for tires was taken along. The old Ford had weak "legs" and before the eight-hour (6 to 2) trip was over had set a record of nine flat tires. After having patched eight, Henry let the ninth one, a blow-out, have it, albeit in a whisper: "Damn it!" It was one of the few expletives he was ever heard to utter. John, hearing the expression, said to Eric, "It's about time!" The return trip homeward, after leaving John at Concordia, did not improve spirits. After healing several more flat tires, the family arrived in Greensboro past midnight, well into the next day. It was Henry's only trip by automobile to Conover during his son's four-year stay at the college.

In Walter he had a problem almost similar to what he himself had experienced. During the summer, while home from preparatory school in Fort Wayne, Walter conducted himself in a way that frequently incurred his father's disapproval. This brought on friction. One evening Walter took the family car, property of the Mission Board, to date a young lady from Bessemer City, five miles east of Greensboro. On his way home Walter drove recklessly and hit a telephone pole. The automobile's radiator was broken and two front wheels were crushed. Walter left the car at the scene and walked home. The next morning he told his father about the accident. Henry was quite upset and the two exchanged harsh words.

It was not the first incident of its kind. Strained feelings between the two had been building up for some time. During one of the hassles Henry had ordered

Walter: "Either obey the rules here and take correction, or pack up your belongings and get out!" To back up his threat, he called the police to have his son ejected from the house. Fortunately, the incident did not lead to the estrangement of father and son, nor did Walter leave home.

Eric's turn came next. One day Henry gave him a fierce tongue lashing and tried to impress the lesson with a severe whipping. "Try out the world and see whether it's easier to live there than at home," he shouted to his son. Eric packed a bag and started toward Bessemer. The closer evening came, the better home looked to him. He knew that genuine love was there, and before darkness descended he turned around and went home.

John likewise had an experience with the punitive side of his father's tight discipline. While at Conover, he was regarded as a good student. His grades were always very acceptable and he gave his professors no difficulties. However, in his senior year of high school he fell in love with a young lady in the town. Although his school work did not especially decline in quality, one of John's professors, Carroll O. Smith, was worried that Latin might lose out in competition with Susie. Without informing John, Smith wrote Henry to tell him about his son's declining academic performance. Such news startled Henry, for he demanded diligent application to school work. He wrote John and urged him to come home immediately to discuss matters. The letter contained bus fare — a most unusual act on the part of his father. The outcome of the visit was that, at the age of seventeen, John was laid over the family table and received his last strapping.

These incidents, while not daily occurrences, pointed to the pietistic and autocratic disciplinary attitude of the father in relation to his children. Henry's philosophy toward his children was: "As long as you put your feet under my table, you will take your orders from me." Helen did very little correcting of the children, particularly of the boys after they had reached the age of puberty. Whatever the children had done wrong during the day was reported to Henry at night, and he took what he considered appropriate action at such times. If a physical correction was needed, he would even arouse the culprit out of sleep.

All members of the family were expected to participate in the evening meal. The seating of the family at table was in accordance with German custom. Henry sat at the head, and Helen at the foot of the table. To his right sat Esther, and to his left Henry Richard. Mary Ann sat next to Esther; Eric sat next to Henry Richard. Irene sat near Mary Ann and close to mother; and John, when at home, sat next to Eric. Practically all of the cooking was done in one pot. One of the favorite dishes, served at least once a week, was curry and rice. The curry sauce, highly spiced, was flavored with a sparse admixture of chicken, beef, or fish. Even if one did not like the food, he or she had to eat it. Father saw to that. One evening Esther had received her portion and could not eat everything. Henry spied her reluctance and with very strong measures forced her to eat every morsel. Thirty minutes after the meal, Esther became violently ill. Henry was greatly disturbed, for he knew that he was responsible for her sudden sickness. Despite his rigidity in applying rules, he never again forced a child to eat. He had a heart, even for his own.

The evening meal ended with the reading of a devotion and the Lord's Prayer. When Henry was absent, Helen led the devotional period. The parents considered this moment of the day a very serious matter, a spiritual experience for all. Since the evening meal was very punctual, to fit into Henry's busy schedule, it always ended about the time that the train from Raleigh to Greensboro was scheduled for the Benbow Road Crossing with an accompanying shrill whistle. The tracks were a good half-mile from the campus, but the whistle could be heard that far. During one of the devotion periods, as the family was praying the Lord's Prayer, Irene heard the whistle of the train and suddenly imitated it with a loud "Wooooooooooo, Woooooo, Wooooooooooo!" The solemnity of the moment broke into a period of hilarious laughter. Henry was not as quick with the rod for the girls as he was for the boys, and Irene escaped with a dose of rhetorical wrath.

Henry never played with his children. Other fathers went fishing and hiking and played ball with their sons, but Henry was too busy for such diversion. The children played with the students of the college and with some of the youth of the neighborhood — all Blacks. Such conditions did not contribute to a very closely knit family, and the effects were readily apparent. By the early forties, every one of the seven children was married and away from home, except for Henry Richard, who was in the U.S. Air Force during World War II; he did not marry until after the conflict. Walter and Mary Ann married without the knowledge of their parents. In the case of Mary Ann, it was a genuine fear of her father, for she had fallen in love with a young man who was not a Lutheran, and she felt that her father would never give her permission to marry him.

Nevertheless, Henry loved his children, and apart from some chafing under his stern discipline, family life in the Nau household was a happy experience. Henry was, in fact, capable of deep feeling. John became more keenly aware of this on the occasion of his marriage to Johanna Hasenkampf. The bride's pastor, Martin W.H. Holls, became ill, and Henry was asked to perform the ceremony. As the young couple stood before him in St. John's Church, New Orleans, Henry was so moved that he forgot the name of his new daughter-in-law. "It's Johanna!" whispered John. After the wedding he told Helen that he would never consent to preside at the marriage of any of his other children, for it was too deep an emotional experience.

When he received the news that his daughter Esther had died eleven days after the birth of her first-born, Henry wept openly. When his son Eric was seriously injured in a fall from a theater marquee while working in Mebane, North Carolina, and remained in a coma for three weeks, Henry spent endless hours at his bedside. When his son John was troubled with a bleeding ulcer and needed a longer rest for therapy and recovery, Henry invited him to come to Greensboro with his family to spend as much time as he needed at his home. As one of his colleagues expressed it in later years to a member of his family: "All children of the world meant as much to him as his own children, and his own children meant as much to him as all the children in the world."

As part of the household routine, Saturday afternoon and evening were spent in town to buy necessities for the family, particularly clothing. Henry did not care for shopping, but he did enjoy the hot dogs and hamburgers served in a small shop, the California Fruit Stand, located on South Elm Street. There he would wait for Helen and the children. At times when he needed a haircut, he went to a barber shop manned by Blacks.

When the family reached home after the Saturday outing, members talked about what they had seen and what they had bought. One Saturday evening, during the family conversation, Henry asked the children what they knew about Greta Garbo. In amazement Esther asked her father, "Where did you learn about Greta Garbo, Papa? She is a movie star!" He answered, "I must make a confession. While waiting for Mama, instead of enjoying a hamburger or hot dog, I have occasionally spent money attending a low-priced movie." The family was perplexed and astonished to learn that Henry would even as much as entertain the idea of attending a movie. They realized more and more that Papa was a many-sided and complex individual, and also human.

Henry took no vacation, as vacations went, during his early years of service at Immanuel. He was at the college and seldom, even in the summer, took a day off from his everyday obligations. It was his own choice. Although he complained even to the Board in St. Louis, he loved to be around whenever work was done on the campus. His brother Conrad urged him to take some time off to come to Ridgeway. He replied, "It's impossible!" When he received an invitation to preach, he considered it a duty to discharge, without thought of extra time for vacation. His brother in Wisconsin, J. Henry, would invite him to spend some time in the area, but Henry would go only when asked to speak at various gatherings about mission endeavors. To spend a day or a week in simple relaxation and play was not in his blood. He might sacrifice an hour or so, while on a lecture circuit, to do a little fishing, but even such indulgence was a rarity.

Henry enjoyed raising vegetables. One day while working in his garden, he noticed a limousine coming up the dirt drive leading to the front of his residence. He knew no one was at home, since Helen had gone shopping and the children were visiting friends. Somewhat apprehensive about the identity of his distinguished visitors who were sitting in a luxury car driven by a liveried chauffeur, Henry walked to the front of the house to greet his guests. Dressed in overalls, he approached the car and saw two well-dressed gentlemen step out. When they saw Henry, they undoubtedly mistook him for part of the maintenance staff, for they inquired of him where they might meet the president of Immanuel Lutheran College, Dr. Henry Nau. He suggested that they make themselves comfortable on the front porch swing while he called the venerable doctor. Quickly he walked to the rear of the house, hurried through the back porch and kitchen to the upstairs bedroom. He removed his overalls, took a hurried "Dutch" bath, put on his suit, and walked to the front door and opened it. Cordially he invited his guests to come in and introduced himself as Henry Nau, the president of Immanuel Lutheran College. The visitors were members of the Board of Education of the state of North Carolina. To their surprise they noticed that, although the man speaking with them was dressed in a suit, he was indeed the same man who greeted them in overalls when they arrived. Henry explained that he did not wish to sit with them in his unbecoming attire and therefore had quickly changed from gardener to president. Henry failed to realize that quality of character and training are not determined by style of garment.

During these years Henry remained a healthy and durable individual. Only one time was he bedridden. He developed a kind of rheumatic condition in his knee. It appeared all at once and tested his small reserve of fortitude and patience for about six summer weeks. His left knee swelled so that he was unable to walk. He was ready to try anything, medically approved or not, to get rid of the malady. One of the nonprescribed medicines was an Indian ointment that was reputed to possess miraculous powers of healing. Eric and John, several times a day, had the task of applying this ointment. Once Eric applied the ointment a bit too freely. Henry screamed and leaped high off the bed. Since Henry was scarcely in shape to administer the leather strap, Eric got off with a tongue lashing. John, who had never before seen his father engage in such a high jump, stood by the door and laughed to himself. The propulsive power of the ointment was directly traceable to the fact that it was ninety percent alcohol. Less subject to analysis was the disappearance of Henry's arthritis. It went as mysteriously as it had come. Neither Henry nor his physician could offer a satisfactory explanation, but Henry had no further difficulty with arthritis for the rest of his life.

In 1932 Henry's mother, Katherine, died at the age of sixty-eight and was buried in Ridgeway, North Carolina. During his years at Immanuel, Henry had contacted a colony of German Lutheran farmers located in Ridgeway. These people were close to him, since their philosophy of hard work was similar to his. He often went to preach in their small rural church. Later on, in the early 1930's, John Moebius, a friend of Henry's from seminary days, took a pastorate at Ridgeway, where Henry broke with his customary concentration on work and spent many a happy day socializing with his neighbor. Also in the vicinity was Henry's brother Conrad, who had married a girl from Ridgeway and was tending a farm there. Although their mother had lived in the United States from 1926 to 1932, she had learned to speak very little English. Henry and Conrad agreed that Katherine should be buried in the cemetery of St. Paul Lutheran Church. As Henry explained to his children: "Grandmother will feel more at home on resurrection morning in the company of those who speak the German language."

CHAPTER 14

Henry Nau's interests were many, but what intrigued and motivated him most was the mission outreach of the church. This was his life. He had read avidly the admirable study by Frank J. Lankenau, *The World is Our Field*. In this work Lankenau encouraged Christians to use as much business acumen in their missionary endeavors as possible. The possibility excited him, and he wrote:

> The Lord God rules the world and especially His Church. While we, there-
> fore, should not wait for special indications of the Lord's will, we should
> also not ignore them when clearly seen. I have never believed that the Lord
> does not give special indications. We did that in starting our mission among
> the Tamil-speaking people in India and have been blessed in doing so.

Now appeared another indication.

As early as 1928 Henry had discussed with Christopher Drewes, executive director of the Mission Board of the Evangelical Lutheran Synodical Conference, the possibility of starting mission work in Africa. Blacks in the southeastern field and elsewhere had not only talked about this possibility but had gathered $6,000 to finance an exploratory trip into Africa to learn whether the Lutheran Church could find virgin lands in which to spread the gospel. Little did Henry realize that the arrival of a young man from Nigeria, West Africa, in 1928, would change his entire life and provide the opportunity for a new venture.

Jonathan Udoe Ekong had been sent by his people, the Ibesikpo of Nigeria, to get the ear and confidence of an American church body and to persuade it to come to their spiritual rescue. On arrival in America he approached Methodists, Presbyterians, and Baptists. Denomination made no difference to him. That the group be Christian was all that mattered. But from all these Christian bodies he received, as with one voice, the answer, "Impossible!"

Time passed, and Ekong came to Salisbury, North Carolina. There he attended Price High School under the supervision of Livingston College. One day he read in a Negro newspaper that Lutherans were contemplating the establishment of a mission in Africa. The very next Sunday, Jonathan attended a Lutheran church of black people pastored by Felton Vorice, a graduate of Immanuel Lutheran College. Coincidentally, Mission director Drewes was present at the service and Vorice presented Ekong and his request to him. Both men would feel forever that they had seen God's footprints in the little church that day.

For many years Drewes had nursed the thought of starting a mission in Africa and had made extensive and careful investigations. He overflowed with eagerness to hear an appeal for the gospel directly from an African's lips. Ekong was just as eager to find a white man aglow with the wish and hope of starting work in his country.

Drewes placed Ekong's request before the Mission Board of the Synodical Conference. Ekong fully understood the situation and knew that the Synodical Conference would need time to come to a decision, but he had difficulty explaining the delay to his people in Africa. They charged him with having forgotten them and accused him of ingratitude. He took their abuse in stride and in his correspondence with them pleaded for understanding.

The Missionary Board made inquiries into the Nigerian conditions, and results at first glance seemed unfavorable to Ekong's cause. The Qua Iboe mission, begun by British laypeople in 1887 under the leadership of Samuel A. Bill, claimed the Ibesikpo country as its territory, with exclusive rights to conduct mission work there. Yet a map issued by that mission showed neither a mission station nor a preaching place in that country. The objection was, however, serious enough to cause further study of the matter and postponement of the decision.

The appeal from Africa became more insistent. "Thousands of people are crying for bread from heaven, and we will be satisfied with crumbs which fall from your table," came the cry. Encouraged by Ekong's recommendation of Lutheranism, his people in Africa began to identify themselves as the United Lutheran Church in Ibesikpo and expressed the desire to be instructed in the teachings of the Lutheran church.

In the fall of 1932 Ekong left Price High School for Immanuel Lutheran College to prepare for the Christian ministry, with the aim to serve his people in Nigeria. He was of medium height, with very dark skin. Tribal marks were on his face, and his two front upper teeth had been filed to a point. He spoke a broken English, was timid in his approach, and dressed without distinction.

By coincidence, the superintendent of the Synodical Conference mission to black people in the eastern part of the United States happened to be on the campus the day that Jonathan arrived. After Ekong had been ushered into the president's office, the superintendent and Henry lost no time in subjecting the young man to a searching cross-examination. In machine gun fashion they fired questions at one who soon felt more victim than guest in a strange land.

Why had Ekong joined the Lutheran Church in Salisbury? Why had he come to Immanuel Lutheran College from Livingston College? Why did he want the Lutheran Church to begin mission work in Africa? Was there any other mission in Nigeria? Why did his people want to have nothing to do with the Qua Iboe mission which had been working in the Ibibio country?

To these and many more questions of a related nature Ekong was expected to give satisfactory answers. Scarcely able to speak English, Ekong naturally failed to impress his interrogators, and they were doubtful whether they should keep him at Immanuel. Nevertheless, Henry during the proceedings had developed further feeling for the man and assigned him to a room with a bed. Ekong, without showing what may have been going on in his soul, but certainly weary and depressed, walked upstairs to be alone with his thoughts. Henry likewise had some pondering to do that night. He had always been proud of his ability to fit himself into another's shoes. Not so this day. The cross-examination he had helped administer reminded him of the one he himself had experienced years earlier in New York. That one contributed to his redemption, but what had they gained from the grilling of this Nigerian? And what had it done to the victim? The indignity and futility of the whole thing stabbed so deeply into Henry's mind that he was ashamed of the manner in which he had proceeded in the interview. He was resolved to make amends.

A friendship between Henry and Ekong grew from day to day. Henry was with him almost constantly. While this was a sign of his growing affection for him, it was also an opportunity for him to learn Efik, the native tongue of the Ibibios. Ekong taught so well that in a relatively short time Henry was able to converse intelligently with Ekong in that tongue. Henry in his turn helped Ekong improve his English. In the cementing of their close relationship, based initially on their mutual linguistic interests, both men learned how love of the Lord develops into forgetfulness of self.

In 1934 Henry wrote about his new-found friend:

> The first impression of Jonathan soon wore off. In the weeks and months to come I had ample opportunity to observe him closely. He was different from most of the other boys; hence, he attracted attention whether he wanted it or not. Without pushing himself into the foreground, he was always there when somebody was wanted and needed. Ever ready and willing to cooperate with school authorities, he found work about the college which no other boy saw or thought of. He sensed when volunteers were wanted and was on the spot before the call came. Not familiar with slipshod ways of work, when he had once laid his hand to the plow he would keep it in hand till the work was finished and well executed.
>
> In his studies he had a very poor foundation, and the necessity of having to pursue his studies in a foreign tongue altogether different from his mother tongue in grammar and syntax presented a great difficulty. His organs of speech have lost their pliability owing to the fact that he took up the study of English too late in life, and he must acquire by diligence and perseverance what others could pick up in passing. Having, however, come from Africa with a definite goal in view, he has a high purpose and with extraordinary determination is bent upon achieving it. Hence, no driving, no admonition on the part of his teachers is necessary. His studies is people, and the task of earning a few dollars to meet certain necessities of life occupies him completely. He has gained the good will and love of his school mates and teachers by his reliability, helpfulness, and cleanliness, physical and moral.

In his words about Jonathan, Henry offered a look into himself, for this friendship gave Henry a new perspective on his life vicariously. It brought an end to the boredom of administrative work at Immanuel and held the hope of beginning a new adventure in a strange country where Henry had never been.

Henry's praise of Jonathan also highlighted the virtues he espoused and admired. During his stay at Immanuel Lutheran College, Jonathan received his last money order, in the amount of ten English pounds, from the people of Ibesikpo. Under the Nigerian's very careful management it lasted for six months, but there was no prospect of getting any more from home. Yet Jonathan continued to need such things as clothes and books. With quick determination he went to the *Daily News* in Greensboro and asked for a paper route. After overcoming some difficulties, he joined the great army of paper carriers. Although he was no match for his slick-tongued, wily patrons, and although paper-carrying was no gold mine, he stuck to it, never missed a payment of his bill to the paper, and earned a few dollars each month for himself. In wind and storm and rain Ekong trotted the streets of Greensboro early in the morning while others still slept. There was never a complaint, never a request for help.

Finally, after receiving a pathetic letter from home, Ekong asked Henry: "Is there nothing that can be done until the final decision is made? My people are dying and are dying fast. No time is to be lost. Can no help be provided? If no missionary can be sent, perhaps books can be sent."

Jonathan's remarks forced Henry to request the Mission Board to send all types of books — sermon books, prayer books, catechisms, Bible histories and the like — to Ibesikpo.

Ekong carried the burden of his people in Africa. Often disappointed, he looked confidently into the future believing that his people's cause was the cause of Christ and was, therefore, borne by hands mightier and more resourceful than his own. Henry's sympathy for Ekong rose to high regard and admiration. This young man from Africa was, in his eyes, a shining example of the power of Christ manifested in a weak vessel. The more Henry's regard and admiration for Ekong grew, the greater was his dissatisfaction with the slowness and hesitancy of the Mission Board to follow the command of the Lord given to the Christian Church: "Go ye." He expressed his feeling that there was in the Ibesikpo country an immense opportunity, a wide open door, in the sense that the country was open and safe for the missionary to come and go as he pleased. There was a people willing to be instructed, with the prospect of gathering large numbers and of establishing within a generation an indigenous Lutheran Church — all was there if the church would but go. Henry's susceptibility to extreme agitation had moved into high gear.

As months passed and the African appeal came through more clearly, Henry expressed even more freely his philosophy of mission. He never sanctioned the idea of entering into a territory of another established mission. Yet he felt that a church or mission society had no right to claim an area for its work if it was not energetically pursuing actual evangelization of the people. He remembered the start of Tamil work in India. The German Leipzig Mission Society had raised serious objections to the coming of the missionaries from the Lutheran Church-Missouri Synod and considered them as ruthless intruders. But their fears were unfounded, for the first mission station of the Mission Board of the Missouri Synod was more than 100 miles away from the Leipzig group. Henry recollected that a missionary of the London Mission, with headquarters in England, who was stationed at Tiripatur in the North Arcot District, considered Krishnagiri in the Salem District his mission field, for he visited Krishnagiri once a year.

Nau was convinced that the Lord was pointing the way to Ibesikpo:

> . . . I see how the Lord points our footsteps to Ibesikpo to serve Him. . . . I venture to project my thoughts into the future, and without speculation can see how our future work in Ibesikpo may have a bearing upon our possible participation in opening up the great unoccupied field of Central Africa to Christ. Nigeria, which borders on Lake Chad, offers one of the highways into the heart of Africa.

Aware that mission activity required courage, total dedication, and personal sacrifice, Henry felt that especially Nigeria called for an elite corps. There were those who would welcome the challenge of the unknown for the sake of Christ. Obstacles would themselves be an enticement; difficulties, a source of strength; sacrifice, a privilege and honor out of love for God and for the lost. Nigeria called for those who preferred to leave hearth and home to go after a lost sheep whose bleat could be but faintly heard through the howling desert sand. Such service of the Lord could tolerate no fear of loneliness. Convinced that Nigeria was a training ground for the church's best, Henry exhorted: "By all means let us welcome this call which came to us through Jonathan Udo Ekong and his people."

Henry took every opportunity to inspire his church for this unique privilege to spread the gospel:

> Someone has said, if the heart of Africa is to be won for Christ, it is to be done by Africans. This seems to be true and reasonable. North Africa has been won for Islam by North Africans. . . . Why should not Africans be able to render a similar service to Christ? They have shown great possibilities in Uganda. Everything speaks in their favor: climate, mode of living, language, ease of travel, and contact with their fellow countrymen. The Lord should lead us to Africa to train the white pioneer missionary. He also surely needs us there to find the assistance of the pioneer African missionary without whom little could be done anywhere in Africa.

Yet Henry was a realist. In retrospect he admitted: "Only a madman would have attempted a new mission enterprise under the circumstances prevailing when the call (to Nigeria) first came to us." There were deficits in every treasury, and he had pondered the propriety of advocating a mission enterprise as challenging and demanding as the one in Africa. Yet the call came again and again and seemed to gain momentum in its urgency. But mission work was serious business and would require money and more money. He therefore demanded that a careful investigation be made before undertaking such a program. He quoted often the admonition of a German director of missions, whose family name was Johannsen: "In mission work we must calculate finances as if the whole work depends upon such calculating. Then we must so believe the promises of the Lord that we forget all our calculating, as if all of our success depends upon nothing else but His gracious promise."

Of course, no one knew better than Henry that caution in financial matters and cold calculation had their place, but they had never started a mission, would never start a mission, and would never promote a missionary enterprise. Mere calculation was death to any mission endeavor. Henry agreed partially with Franz Lankenau's statement that the Christian crusade in the first century began not with going but with waiting. But he knew that the Apostles, after waiting for the ascension of the Lord and Pentecost, received the gift of the Spirit, with the command to go to all areas of the world. "The spirit of calculation was totally absent at that time," said Henry. "The Great Depression must never deter us from the challenge. We must possess the genius of transforming the barely possible into actuality." His rhetoric intensified: "We are convinced that God wants us to come to the rescue of the people of Ibesikpo, now starving for want of spiritual food; and if we are confident that with Him nothing is impossible, we shall be able to laugh in the face of the depression and in spite of it begin the work in the knowledge that we have on our side a factor with whom the impossible becomes not only practical but imperative."

·In venturing such a philosophy of mission, he had thrown down the gauntlet and was prepared to do his part. He lived by the words of the poet: "Set on fire our hearts' devotion / with the love of thy dear name, / till o'er every land and ocean / tongues and lives thy cross proclaim."

By 1934 Henry was absolutely convinced that the Lutheran Church-Missouri Synod and the Synodical Conference must undertake the work of bringing Christ to the people in the Cross River Valley in Nigeria, Africa. As for himself he had no clear vision as to how he would fit into the plan. India was never out of his mind, but would he ever return to that great land of opportunity? "God will direct," was the faith of the one whom the Spirit inspired with the Great Commission.

CHAPTER 15

"Who will do the exploratory work?" churchmen asked when faced with the African challenge. One choice seemed a natural. In Henry the church had a man prepared by God in the crucible of life. The preparation had started in India, continued in Germany, become more intense in New Orleans, and apparently found completion at Immanuel Lutheran College.

Schooled in facing the will of God without question but the will of men with reservation, Henry had fought the closed-door policy tenaciously.

That battle had helped him see the pros and cons of sharing the good news with everyone. At the same time he had wrestled with problems of finance and of administration, and each of these had tested his mettle. His friendship with Ekong and his linguistic talents appeared to be God's own way of preparing Henry for a new assignment. In 1905 he was needed in India; now in 1935 he seemed to be just the man to explore the possibilities of mission work in Africa. Yet when the Synodical Conference selected the members of the exploratory group, which Henry had strongly advocated, he was not included. Whatever went through his mind when he discovered that he was left off the exploratory committee was never expressed, but the experiences of the past must have whispered that God had other work for him to do than visit Africa. He had always wanted to return to India. Perhaps he might again be needed there.

Then lightning out of the blue struck in November 1934, when Edwin Wilson, one of the members chosen to explore Africa's possibilities for a new mission field, was unable to go because of other commitments. The committee then chose Henry to join Emmanuel Albrecht and Otto C. Boecler. Henry was almost beside himself. He would go to Nigeria to visit Ekong's people. Word spread rapidly in Greensboro and throughout the Carolinas that Dr. Nau, as he was known to thousands of Blacks, was chosen as one of the three to explore the mission possibilities in Nigeria. The uncertainties in Henry's future disappeared. He was most eager to see what many had come to call the "Dark Continent." The exploratory group completed all preparations during the month of December and sailed from New York on January 4, 1935.

The closer the party came to the tropics, the more Henry enjoyed himself. He observed all the scenery and was reminded of the years he spent in the tropical climate of India. Many a time he was heard to exclaim, "This is just the way it looked in India!" He kept a daybook so that he could accurately report all that he saw and heard and could record his own impressions. He wanted everyone back home, especially the members of the Mission Boards of the Synodical Conference and of the Missouri Synod, to know the facts. He reveled in meeting the people. He enjoyed the climate and food, and detailed everything connected with life along the western coastline of Africa. It was a most welcome change from his embattled life as president at Immanuel College.

Henry did not feel quite at home with his traveling companions. Both Albrecht and Boecler were men of different tastes and backgrounds. He was a man of simple ways. His life had been tempered in India for almost ten years under very trying circumstances, and in the South of the United States he had for many years adapted himself to the life style of the Blacks around him. He expected them to be treated with equity, and he demanded no special privileges for himself. His companions, Boecler and Albrecht, were accustomed to more elegant foods and more convenient accommodations for their everyday needs. They had enjoyed the more comfortable life of ministers in the Midwest.

Henry had difficulty interpreting the ship's menu, which listed a half-dozen brands of cheeses. Henry knew only American cheese and Swiss cheese. He also liked *Schmierkaese,* the kind his mother made; it had a decided odor and seemed at times "alive." Albrecht and Boecler, on the other hand, knew the brands of all the cheeses on the menu and had eaten them before.

Nor did matters improve after disembarking in early February. The three men received an invitation to dine on goat and yams at the home of a tribal chief in the African bush village of Afaha. After their arrival at the jungle cottage, they watched the preparation of the goat, which was to be the main course of the evening meal. The whole process of boiling the goat seemed to the visitors to violate all rules of hygiene. Millions of insects and flies hovered over the carcass, yet the preparation went on. Henry had seen things like this before, also in the United States, and he was annoyed that visitors to foreign countries seldom seemed to notice anything but flies and snakes, when there were so many really beautiful things to comment on. When mealtime came, Boecler and Albrecht were unable to eat but Henry enjoyed the meal. He was not about to hurt the feelings of his host and, more important, he knew that boiling the food had made everything eatable.

The committee of three worked untiringly, visiting villages, churches, and congregations and meeting with leaders. The more they heard and the more they saw, the more they were convinced that the call of the Ibibios should be answered quickly. After an eight-week visitation in the bush, Albrecht and Boecler left for America in April, but Henry remained to assist in translating Luther's small Catechism into Efik, the language of the people, and to determine mission expansion in adjoining provinces.

Henry easily made friends with many of the people. They urged him to stay and get the mission under way. That was, of course, impossible, for the Synodical Conference had to make the decision. But Henry knew what question would be uppermost in the mind of the board: "What are the possibilities for mission expansion?" A positive answer would mean that the church back home would grant the wish of the Africans.

Henry lost no time investigating the matter. He arranged an exploratory trip into the adjoining Ogoja province. This would take him to the headquarters of Lake Chad, south of the Sahara Desert. To cover the approximately 150 miles across country he had to walk. Carriers were needed to handle everyday necessities. To find these carriers he interviewed about 200 members of the Munchi tribe. These tribesmen were trained from childhood to carry heavy loads on their heads for long distances without removing them. After tedious hours of interview and inspection, he had his required complement of able bodied men.

Henry started his walking excursion into Ogoja in May. The jungle path was just wide enough for the men to walk single file. Meals were cooked along the way, and sleeping accommodations were arranged beforehand with chieftains of the tribes inhabiting the jungles.

Day by day, he learned many things about the people living in the bush. He was especially intrigued by their burial customs. Along the path were many small clearings, covered with crude wooden structures that were filled with cooking and eating utensils hanging from wooden pegs. These were erected as memorials, in the belief that the dead man had use for the same utensils in the afterlife as he had in this life. Each cup, platter, and spoon had holes in it. Henry concluded that this was done to avoid looting.

After a few days on the way he suddenly froze. There at his feet was a 17-foot African python slithering across the jungle path. He thought he had seen a reincarnation of the cobra he had encountered in India.

Once he miscalculated distances between villages. He had traveled an entire day in the jungle without adequate supplies of drinking water. The heat was unbearable. His strength waned. Blind to the substitute resources around him, he saw his life ebbing away. He felt as close to death as he had been at any time in his life. Suddenly, at a turn in the path he caught sight of a very small village. There he found safe drinking water and enjoyed the hospitality of the village chief, who assured him of night lodgings. Although the types of experiences he was having were not entirely new to Henry, he was learning firsthand the misadventures a missionary could expect in the African bush. For himself, he knew that God had spared him for a purpose. Only the purpose was not yet spelled out.

One day Henry met a man who claimed to be a victim of a headhunter. More than likely his encounter with danger was part of the standard bush politics of staking out territory. Attacked from the rear, the African saved his life by turning his head to the side when the attack came. The stroke of the machete was supposed to sever the man's head from his body. Instead it struck his lower jaw. The wound was severe, but the man's life was spared.

Farther on, Henry had the opportunity to visit a leper colony. This institution of mercy was maintained by Methodist Christians. Since leprosy was very prevalent in the bush, he thought that a like effort might be made among the Ibesikpo people.

After his preliminary exploration, Henry was convinced that the trip was well worth the time and effort. Expansion was indeed possible. This conclusion, combined with the factor of need, filled Henry with fresh resolution.

In the summer of 1935 he returned to the United States to be met by his son, John, in New York City. Together they traveled to Cleveland, Ohio, where he gave a full report of the committee's findings in Nigeria. At that convention he urged the Lutheran Church-Missouri Synod to do all in its power to accept the call of the Ibesikpo people and to send missionaries.

At no time had Henry expressed any personal interest in going to Nigeria as a missionary. Indeed, had he been asked the question at Cleveland, he would have responded with strong mixed feelings. Yet less than a year after the Cleveland convention and the decision to begin work in the bushland of Ibesikpo, Henry and Helen received their assignment as the first missionaries of the Synodical Conference of the Lutheran Church to work in Nigeria. Their minds traveled back to the time in India when they moved from Krishnagiri to Trivandrum to be the first representatives of their Synod to work among the Pariahs.

Henry was thought to be too advanced in years for permanent work in Africa. His board therefore asked him to spend at least enough time to lay the groundwork and to begin organizing the mission. But from Henry's own standpoint he was fifty-three years young. Others felt that the members of the synodical Mission Board never appreciated the vitality, spirit, and power of the man. He was, in fact, a riddle to most of them.

Once having made his decision, Henry could scarcely wait to leave. Spirit-filled, he was always in a mood of anticipation when an opportunity for a new mission venture came. A leave of absence from his duties as president of Immanuel Lutheran College was quickly arranged. Arrangements for the family posed no special problems. As the years passed, Walter, Eric, and Mary Ann had married and despite adverse economic conditions had established their own homes. John was completing his final year of theological studies at Concordia Seminary, St. Louis, Missouri, and was asked by the Mission Board to take up the slack at Immanuel by teaching during his father's absence. Esther had employment. Only Henry and Irene, the two youngest, depended on support from their parents.

During a meeting in New York, called by the Mission Board prior to his departure for Nigeria, Henry discussed the mission policies to be followed in Africa. He remembered the difficulties he had had in India when often he had been reprimanded for taking a step without first consulting the board. He had definite ideas of how the work should progress among the Ibesikpo people, and he now wanted more freedom of action. To the credit of members on the board, for this venture Henry was to have more freedom of decision on the spot and he was to handle financial arrangements as he saw fit. By this time, not only members of his Mission Board but also administrators in the Missouri Synod, as well as Synodical Conference leaders, regarded Henry as their best missionary bargain. He was of immense value in the field, he indulged himself in no luxuries, and practiced prudent fiscal responsibility in the work. If there was a way to save money, Henry would find it. Monies entrusted for the work came from average-income Christians, and Henry felt that good stewardship meant not only that Christians were to give generously, but that administrators had the responsibility to spend their gifts wisely. Henry always took the cheapest travel accommodations and ate the cheapest food. When, however, the kingdom's work required immediate action, financial or otherwise, he did not want to be under duress to wait for permission. It would often be weeks in coming, precious time could be lost, and the work of the gospel seriously impaired.

Henry also put the problem of his dependent children, Henry Richard and Irene, before the board. Both were in their teens, and it was important to Henry that appropriate arrangements be made immediately. A member of the board, after listening to Henry's plea for his two children, asked him, "Don't you trust God to take care of your children?" Henry replied, "I trust God, but in this case I am dealing with men, and I demand an answer."

The arrangements, which satisfied Henry, specified that his son Henry Richard would be maintained at Guilford College near Greensboro, North Carolina, and his daughter Irene would stay in the home of a Lutheran family, the Gerhardt Bindigs of Salem Church in Buffalo, New York.

Henry's preparations to depart for Africa to start the first Lutheran activity among the Ibesikpo people were now almost complete. What he failed to realize was the impact of his enterprise on the thousands of black people in the Synodical Conference of the Lutheran Church. Their hopes and dreams were now to be fulfilled. The good news of God's love in Jesus Christ was about to be sent to some of their own people in Africa. The morning before leaving Greensboro, he was aroused from sleep by the sound of song. He looked at Helen, who also had been awakened by the same sounds. "We cannot be in heaven, Mama, or are we? The singing sounds like that of angels."

Helen realized that the singing was coming from the lawn south of the president's home. She looked out of the window and in a startled voice cried out, "Henry! Henry! Come to the window and see the hundreds of people gathered outdoors singing songs!"

"People wouldn't gather on our lawn this early in the morning to sing spirituals and other religious songs," he answered, in a tone that said, "You're crazy."

"Yes it is!" insisted Helen. "Come to the window and see for yourself!"

Henry went to the window and saw a crowd of Blacks singing. They let him know how deeply they appreciated his courage and his willingness to go to Africa to spread the good news. Henry and Helen dressed quickly, went to the southside porch of the house, and received the applause of hundreds of Blacks, not only of those from the church, but of many black citizens of Greensboro who had learned of his decision. All were bidding them *bon voyage* and the blessings of God on their mission to their brothers and sisters. Henry and Helen, warmed by the love of the people among whom they labored, thanked them profusely for their expressions of love and concern.

Before his departure from New York, a special farewell service was arranged in the chapel of the Lutheran Intermission Society. Lewis Henze, mission director of the Missouri Synod's Atlantic District, gave the sermon. With blessings and prayers, the worshipers entrusted Henry and Helen to the Director of the Great Commission.

CHAPTER 16

In March 1936 Henry and Helen Nau left for Nigeria. The *Amstelkerk*, a Dutch ship of passenger and freight accommodations, was their home for four weeks. During this time they skirted the western coast of Africa into the area of the Gold Coast, arriving at Lagos in the middle of April. Then the ship proceeded to Port Harcourt. There, April 21, she dropped anchor, after moving upstream through narrow, shallow, and winding channels, which were at their deepest six fathoms. Often the ship scraped the bottom of the river. On disembarkment, Henry and Helen were greeted by two representatives of the Ibesikpo people, who were overjoyed to receive into their midst the first Lutheran missionaries from America. The immigration authorities, however, were less enthusiastic.

In Lagos, Henry had received the startling news that he had to deposit 120 English pounds in order to ensure his departure from the country should he become ill or, for other reasons, mainly political, be expelled from the country. Henry quickly computed that the amount required was the equivalent of $600. That would take every cent he had. An agent of the Woermann Shipping Line consented, however, to an arrangement calling for a small deposit on the return ticket and a certification to the government of Nigeria that Henry's shipping line would guarantee his and Helen's return to America in case of emergency. Henry was overjoyed when the immigration officer in Port Harcourt accepted this solution.

There were no baggage carriers in Port Harcourt, so Henry was forced to take care of the transportation himself. In a torrential thunderstorm, with baggage piled high on a truck that had been engaged at the railroad station, Henry and Helen huddled close together to warm themselves and proceeded to make the final miles to their first home in the African bush, the village of Nung Udoe. The driver of the truck managed to lose his way, causing some anxious moments. But about midnight they drove up to their bush home, which had been constructed by the people for the missionaries.

The Naus' first night meant a banquet for the mosquitoes. Henry tossed and swatted all night, but comforted himself with the thought that this was much like India.

The mosquitoes played no favorites, and Helen encored: "They were as big and thirsty as this in Travancore."

With the arrival of the new day, Henry and Helen were able to take their first real look at their new home. At that time it was the only American Lutheran home in Nigeria. It stood in the midst of a half-cleared plot of ground that was about eight acres in size. To construct the house, the people used only one type of tool, a bush knife. The entire home was built of material that grew in the jungle. Sticks were put into the ground and then cross-tied with a very tough reed grass as thick as a finger. Dozens of local Christian women then plastered it by hand with mud. The white clay used to finish the house came from a creek not far from the building site. It gave the building a white appearance, in contrast to the yellow coloration of other houses in the area. Palm leaves tied to bamboo poles served as framework for the roof. This kind of construction made the house cooler than one covered with zinc and sealed with timber.

When Helen had finished her tour, she pronounced their new quarters more primitive than the house she had lived in during her early years in India. As for Henry, he admired it as though it were a castle. Ever afterward he assured his visitors that the floor of the house was level with the outside ground, but that it was useless to look for wooden floors. Bare mud, beaten hard and covered with palm mats was the floor. It was no place for high heels, but it was home to him and his helpmeet, and it became their working headquarters.

Two rooms, one of which was used as a bedroom, another as a bathroom, were on one side of the house. On the opposite side, one room served as study and workroom, the other as kitchen. A hallway ran through the center of the cottage. The rooms were furnished with fiber furniture, made locally.

The bathroom was the quaintest room of all. There was no tile floor, no hot and cold water, no built-in bathtub, and no fuel. There was water and plenty of it, from the creek, disinfected for safety's sake with permanganate of potash. The bathtub was movable. Other accessories were placed in order on several kerosene boxes decorated with cretonne.

"You had to be very careful in our bathroom," Helen quipped in her descriptions. "The floor was bare mud and any splashing of water turned the floor into a mire. But you learn quickly to be careful."

Henry and Helen boiled and filtered every drop of drinking water. It came from the creek, the same source used for bathing and washing of clothes and utensils.

For six weeks the Naus slept on narrow, uncomfortable camp cots that were closed in by mosquito nets. After that they bought two mattresses made by a Hausa man in Calabar. The mattresses were placed on springless bedsteads made by local craftsmen. On their first night in these beds they said to each other: "What a blessing to sleep in a bed long and wide enough to turn about and to be far enough away from the mosquito curtains!"

To provide protection against the lethal malarial mosquito, Henry had the paneless windows of his home covered with cheesecloth until proper screens could be made and fitted. He and Helen took liberal doses of quinine to strengthen their bodies against the scourge. The quinine bottle was as much a fixture at meals as salt and pepper shakers in western restaurants.

In the study, a most important area of the home, were two long bamboo shelves. They held stacks of paper, ink, a duplicating machine, typewriter stencils, and other tools. In addition to the materials used for preparation and duplication of Sunday School lessons, there was room for catechisms, Bible histories, and prayer books.

Helen loved flowers. With Henry's help, which was rare, she tried to raise a few ornamental shrubs, and in the back of the house a small American garden. They had very little success with either. The ornamental shrubs in front of the house grew very slowly because they were planted in the wrong season. The vegetable garden in the back of the house was seeded with beans, cucumbers, squash, and tomatoes, which, they thought, would grow in a hot climate. They had not taken into consideration that in Africa millions of pests and insects, in the absence of proper insecticides, made a veritable banquet of everything that sprang up. In retrospect, Henry exclaimed that they had little luck in their farming operations, except for the planting of banana sprouts. These sprouts grew into big banana trees laden with heavy clusters of bananas, in time for the Naus to enjoy them before their tour of duty in Nigeria came to an end.

The farming operations of the local people were relatively simple. In the planting season the women, who did the heavy work in Africa, hurried to their fields, which were annually covered with wild vegetation. They stripped the foliage from the trees, cleared away the underbrush, and began to plant. The tree trunks and limbs were used as supports for the crops. After the harvest had been completed, the fields were returned to the bush. Their staple foods were assaba (a variety of yam unfamiliar to Americans) and palm oil. The only cash income for the people came from the fruit of the palm, which they sold to English traders.

Several pieces of furniture in Helen's house were a novelty to the villagers. They came to visit her so often that Henry and Helen had very little privacy. Finally, Henry decided to raise the wall of the entrance to the house so that his neighbors had to announce themselves before walking in. During their visitations, the people talked about the Naus' work and asked many questions, also about the odd pieces of furniture, especially the ice box. None of them had ever seen a piece of ice. The ice box, operated by kerosene, was the only luxury item in the house. Henry tried to explain its operation, but his inquirers were more interested in the result. They would hold out their hands for a piece of ice and hold it until they were forced by the cold to drop it. Then they considered the ice box an instrument of some evil spirit. Finally, curiosity gave way to caution and some of the people never returned to the house. Since they had been coming in droves, the Naus were not displeased with this decline in interest.

By this time the Naus had become adjusted to another source of annoyance. During their first weeks they lost sleep over the beating of tom-toms. The monotonous beat of the drums seemed especially vehement when the moon was full. But after a time they became accustomed to the rhythm and even enjoyed it.

As a pioneer missionary, Henry tried to emulate St. Paul in becoming "all things to all people." Soon word spread that he was not only a capable translator and evangelist, judge and administrator, but also a medical adviser. Henry had developed an association with a young Methodist minister and doctor, whose family name was Morris. This gentleman had founded a dispensary and staffed it with native assistants. He and Henry worked to dispel the fears prevalent in the bush. Their friendship made it possible for Henry to take his own people to the dispensary, not only for the yaws, a common disease in the bush of Africa, but also for injuries received at the time of the harvesting of the palm fruit.

To harvest the palm nuts, barefooted workers would climb the tall trunks of the palm with the dexterity of monkeys. Occasionally, however, a workman would lose his footing and suffer a severe stomach injury from the fall. When news of such an accident reached Henry, he would hurry to the scene with his station wagon, place the injured man flat on the floor of the wagon, and have him raise his legs to the roof. He would then drive his patient over the bumpy bush road to the dispensary. On the way, due to the severe bumping and the position of the legs relative to the body, the intestines would recede. Those who had assisted Henry in placing the injured man into the car and who were riding with him would see the intestines gradually disappear. They thought the white man was a magician. On arrival at the clinic, Dr. Morris and Henry would perform the operation. They saved many a life in this way.

Other scourges in the bush were leprosy and the tsetse fly. The latter induced sleeping sickness in humans and brought death to cows and horses.

The killing of twins was common among the Ibibios. They regarded them as a bad omen, and mothers who felt themselves cursed by such a birth would not hesitate to destroy their double offspring. Whenever Henry received news of the birth of twins in the bush, he would rush to the mother's side and try to persuade her to give him the twins. If successful, he would take the babies home and place them in a basket near the vent pipe of the kerosene-operated ice box, which provided warmth for the tiny, fragile lives during the night. There they were kept until the mother was convinced that the birth of twins was not a curse but a blessing. Then they would be returned to her care.

One of Henry's saddest experiences was the time he received word that twins were born to a woman in Udo. He rushed to the bush dwelling and found the mother more than anxious to give the missionary the twins, for she believed them to be bad luck. He rushed the babies to his house and placed them in a basket. That night the twins were fed, wrapped in a small sheet, and placed on top of the refrigerator. The next morning Henry noticed that both of the infants were dead. One appeared to have died of natural causes, but the other was lying in his own blood. Startled, Henry examined the infant. To his chagrin, he found a palm thorn driven into the buttocks of the twin. The murder had already been committed before he had arrived to rescue the infant. Henry, now certain that the parents had killed both of the infants, called the village dispenser, who made a grave in the banana grove and buried them.

Suspicion that the father and mother had killed their offsprings mounted. A complaint was filed with the assistant district officer, who was conducting a court session in a neighboring clan. He ordered a post-mortem examination. Henry hurried back to the grave of the twins, dug up the children, wrapped them each in a piece of cloth, and gave them to the two policemen who had been ordered by the district officer to take the bodies to Dr. Morris at Ituk Mdam. After examining the bodies, Morris certified that the twins had been strangled. The policemen took this report to the assistant district officer, who instituted criminal proceedings against the parents. In the evening the police arrested them and took them to the jail in Udo, where the hearing took place. The judge was an Englishman who had just been transferred from Palestine to Nigeria and knew nothing about the habits and customs of the people. Without questioning anyone in the court, he declared that he had read the written testimony of all parties concerned and in his mind there was at least some doubt as to the guilt of the parents. Unaware of the power of irrational fear, he could not believe that parents could or would take the life of their own offspring.

Since it was the duty of the judge to give the benefit of the doubt to the accused, he acquitted the parents of the charge brought against them. Morris, who was standing next to Henry, whispered into his ear, "Doubt? How could there be any doubt?'' It was a sobering experience for Henry to discover that he could not rely on the strong arm of the government to change the customs of the people and root out the murder of twins. Yet, before they left Africa, Henry saw six pairs of twins saved, and they were toddling about when he and Helen took leave of the continent.

Henry and Helen spent one Christmas in the bush. Their man-servant, Basi, decorated the home with palms and flowers, in lieu of a Christmas tree, a phenomenon unknown in this part of Africa. They arose at seven in the morning, had their breakfast, and then attended church in Nung Udoe. After the service they returned to their home and enjoyed a Christmas dinner consisting of duck, rice, green peas, carrots, and pineapple for dessert. It was more American than African. Their afternoon was broken by an emergency trip to Ituk. A man had fallen from an oil palm. Henry lost no time in rushing to his side with medical assistance, but there was little he could do. The victim died of internal injuries.

In the evening, after returning home, they talked about their loved ones in the States. Their thoughts also drifted to India, where they had celebrated many times the day of God's most precious gift to humanity. Then the day slipped into history — the history of a man and his wife inspired in mission to bring good tidings of great joy.

CHAPTER 17

Henry was on the road constantly, going from school to school and congregation to congregation. He loved his work, but he was not naive. Each continent had its special varieties of trouble, and Henry was well aware of the risks a missionary ran in Africa. Malaria, sleeping sickness, yellow fever, typhoid fever, and other infectious diseases toppled the most stalwart. Henry felt that he and Helen could bring down the appalling mortality rate with quinine and common sense. And he supported his conviction with scripture: "There shall no evil befall thee, neither shall any plague come nigh thy dwelling."

The bush of Ibibio land made an especially deep impression on Henry. It was so dense, he said, that a 200-pound man could jump from a moving train or a low-flying airplane and never hit the earth. The arms of the vines and entanglements of the jungle would cradle and suspend him between heaven and earth.

Violent threats to life in an entire year in the bush probably did not exceed those encountered in a single day at that time on U.S. Highway 66. But one did develop respect for the right of way of the many species of wildlife that inhabited the dense undergrowth. Leopards, both spotted and black, ran along the roads late at night. Generally they were peaceful, but would fight furiously when cornered or wounded. A small tiger cat, as furious as the lynx, also lived in the jungle. It would pillage chicken houses and rob the nests of birds. Large pythons, including the green Mamba and the Asaba, lurked in the jungle. Henry had developed a special technique for dealing with any interference from that source. He would simply roll over it with his car, put the reptile in a box hung on the exhaust of the car, and shoot the poisonous fumes of the exhaust into the box for 23 minutes, after which the python would be limp as a dishcloth. The villagers would then skin it, give Henry the skin as a remembrance, and take the steaks home for dinner.

Elephantiasis was another hazard of the bush country. This disease affected certain abdominal glands and the breasts of women. Their breasts became so bloated and heavy that the women could not stand straight. Men also were grossly disfigured by it.

Ibibio land experienced two seasons, with slow transition from one to the other. The dry season covered the end of November to May, and the rainy season May to November. In November the rains dwindled to almost nothing, and the wind began to blow from the north, bringing with it more and more sand particles from the Sahara Desert. About Christmas the country was wrapped in a bluish haze that dried the lips and throat and left them inflamed. This was the dreaded harmattan. In an open car one did well to wear a duster to protect clothes against the sand. Sand and white dust coated everything in the house. It was like living in a dust bowl for a few weeks. Fortunately this condition did not last long. Uniformly hot weather soon set in again. Water holes, which ordinarily supplied drinking water for the villagers, dried up or became so contaminated that a serious shortage developed. To obtain water for cooking and drinking, the women walked miles to bring water from larger creeks and rivers.

Water is not an unmixed blessing, and abundance of it in Henry's region brought a variety of woes. During the rainy season rheumatism and pneumonia were very prevalent among the nationals, as well as among the resident Europeans. Water brought more mosquitoes, and more mosquitoes brought more malaria and other diseases. In all respects it was an unhealthful season, and everyone was glad when the rains were over. Such changing conditions of wet and dry, sickness and health, compelled Henry to embark on a project that would make history in his village: the digging of a well that would supply pure water at all times.

No one had ever dug a well in this part of Africa. But Henry was not about to go through a repetition of his earlier experience when he thought he would die for lack of drinking water. He had several villagers who were willing to dig, so he procured the equipment and began the work. It was tedious labor but, under Henry's encouragement that they would soon strike water, the workers kept digging. The shaft was now deep enough that it was difficult to see the bottom. Suddenly the workers refused to dig any further. They were not about to disturb Mother Earth and her spirits any further. "The evil spirits of the darkness will get us," they said.

Henry was troubled. It was imperative to get the diggers working again until he struck a vein of water. He thought for a while, and then came up with what he thought might be the answer. He took a chicken and in the presence of the workers let it down to the bottom of the well. Then he aimed an ordinary search light toward the bottom of the shaft and gave the chicken some light. Then he dropped some feed in front of the chicken. As the chicken acclimated itself, it started to peck the earth and the grain. Henry enthusiastically showed the natives that a chicken was not afraid of the darkness at the bottom of the shaft. "You are human beings," he exclaimed. "But it looks as though a little chicken is braver than you." The natives talked to one another, caught the hint, and before long they decided that they were better than chickens and continued their digging.

News soon spread that the "white father" had made water rise out of the earth. One day an important chief came with a large umbrella to Nung Udoe to see the well. He had walked three days to see this wonder. Okon, Henry's servant, was standing at the left side of the chief. The chief looked down the well, then turned to Okon and said, "I see nothing."

Okon took a pebble and threw it into the well. The water at the bottom stirred. The chief in amazement exclaimed, "There it is, there it is, mon, water!" Then the boy and the chief exchanged a question and answer period:

"Is this good water?"
"Yes, that is good water."
"Is this clear water?"
"Yes, this is clear water."
"Is this cool water?"
"Yes, this is cool water."
"Is this sweet water?"
"Yes, this is sweet water."
"Can man drink this water?"
"Yes, man can drink this water."

"Can I drink this water?"

"Yes, you can."

"How will this water come to me?"

"It will come to you right now, see!"

Okon let a bucket down into the well and pulled it up. The chief took the bucketful of water into his hands and sniffed. "This smells good."

The water boy answered, "Yes, this smells good."

"This is clear."

"Yes, it is clear."

The chief took a swallow of water in his mouth and said, "This is cool."

Okon answered, "Yes, it is cool."

The chief took another swallow and said, "This is sweet."

The young man replied, "Yes, this is sweet."

After that the chief drank his fill of the good, cool, sweet water. Then he turned to the houseboy and said, "How did this white man know that he would find water here on top of the hill?"

Okon answered, "That I do not know. But one thing is sure, the white man knew that the water was here."

The chief excitedly remarked, "How? How? The white man knows all things. He even knows where water is in the earth!"

To draw the water from the well, Henry ordered a pump through the United African Company. It took longer to get the pump than to dig the well, but by 1938 the well was in full operation. One afternoon, however, Okon came with the news that the pump was not spitting water anymore. It did not take Henry long to discover why. While Henry and Helen were on vacation in the Cameroons, Okon had entertained numerous visitors with this marvelous contrivance and had pumped the well dry in the demand for encores, and the cast-iron pump finally refused to do any more spitting. After the repair work, a chain and lock assured that the well would always have sufficient water for drinking purposes. The days of demonstration of its spitting power were over.

When Henry arrived in Africa, he found 16 organized congregations among the Ibibio Christians. They were under the spiritual headship of William Akpan of Nung Ukana, a man who enjoyed the respect of his people and whose word and counsel carried weight. He was a fairly well-to-do man, with a little shop on one of the small rivers in Nait. He bought up palm oil and sold it again in Opaho to European traders.

Akpan presided at every communion service held in these churches and ministered to the people without charge, so long as such ministrations did not interfere with his trade. Henry appreciated leaders of such capability, but he observed that their fluency in communication of biblical teaching was not always matched by quality of basic understanding. Many of their listeners believed that heaven could be gained by working out a deal with God. To place the emphasis on faith, with a good life as fruit of the Holy Spirit's work, in place of a bargaining relationship with God, became Henry's consuming effort.

The fighter never lacked opportunity for battles. Spiritism and polygamy quickly became his chief target. Spiritism thrived on fear of a world controlled by good and evil spirits that were thought to be the sources of life's weal and woe. In this fight, he showed more determination than diplomacy. Again and again he discussed the subject of spiritism and the practice of faith healing with a number of chieftains, who served as priests. He was so adamant in his own position that he refused to give ground, even when a number of chiefs opposed him. Helen sensed that they were growing increasingly hostile toward Henry and urged him to back off a bit and negotiate matters when the chieftains had cooled down. "I am afraid for both of us," she said.

Henry also had no sympathy whatsoever, at this time, for polygamy. He was convinced that no Christian could be a polygamist, yet the practice was closely interwoven with the everyday life of the people. He attacked it vehemently, but was not successful in eradicating it. Almost in despair, he stated: "Sometimes it seems so easy to free oneself from a polygamous relationship, and again in other cases it seems impossible." The news of his dealing with polygamy reached the members of the board in St. Louis. In a letter they advised Henry not to be too "legalistic" or "dictatorial" among the natives. He possessed both of these qualities in great measure, but was angered whenever anyone used such terms to describe what he considered his virtues.

On the other hand, whenever he was confronted with problems prevalent in the congregations, he could be patient and forbearing to a degree never exhibited in his dealings with nonmembers. His response to the existence of prayer houses within the Christian community illustrates his attitude well. Because of alleged association of such prayer houses with voodooism, he himself did not tolerate them in congregations under his jurisdiction. However, when a congregation of about 2,000 members organized their own prayer houses in the form of evening devotions, he thought that the question would have to be reconsidered from the Africans' point of view. Gradually he became convinced that such prayer houses would someday exist throughout all the congregations.

In late 1937, after working hard for months with only a few hours of sleep at night, Henry and Helen went on a well-earned vacation. Henry had been on the lookout for an area where missionaries might retreat for a while from the debilitating climate of the African bush. The Cameroons appeared to be the answer. Henry had heard about its invigorating climate and a rest home maintained by several Baptist missionaries in Victoria. At Port Harcourt, Henry stored the station wagon with the United African Company, attended to some other business, including the purchase of a new filtering system, and took Helen aboard the *Wadai* for a most pleasant and welcome trip to the Cameroons, vacationland for tired missionaries.

As they approached the beautiful city of Victoria, they saw the 14,000-foot mountain range known as the Mt. Cameroon reaching into the sky. The shoreline was fringed with coconut palms. Their greenish-brown color stood out against the background of the red roofs that dominated the city.

About to experience one of the few vacations he ever really enjoyed, Henry said to Helen, "We deserve this one." There were no mosquitoes or other insects to speak of. After their earlier long wars with mosquitoes, the few sand flies felt like a reprieve. The daylight hours were very comfortable, and the evenings were cool enough for sweaters. Because of the altitude, ranging from 8,000 feet up, the climate was conducive to the cultivation of strawberries. Henry and Helen thought they had never tasted any so good, for neither of them had eaten any for years.

Vacation time passed quickly, but they had accomplished the purpose of their visit. The less rigorous climate and abundance of rest had helped restore their vitality. As added bonus, they learned from the Baptists how to do mission work more effectively in Africa.

On their return to Nung Udoe, they were greeted by the school children who lined the jungle road for several miles and joyfully acclaimed their return to the tune of various musical instruments.

As in India, Henry realized that responsibility for successful mission work must be assumed by the people among whom it is done. This meant that Africans had to be entrusted with the direction and development of the work. Policy making had to be done on the field, not in an office in New York, Chicago, or St. Louis. In moments of disgust his mission philosophy found expression in the succinct query: "Why is the church, which entrusts the greater things to man in the mission field, namely, the salvation of blood-bought souls, so slow in entrusting also the lesser things to them, the direction of their own work?"

The establishment of an indigenous church remained his objective in Africa. Through official mission channels he urged Stateside congregations to permit Africans to support their own congregations, and to build their own churches and schools, and to staff them with their own people. The church at home should, he felt, supply the necessary know-how through dedicated, consecrated, and fearless missionaries who would act as advisers and not as policy makers.

Henry did in fact see some aspects of indigenous church organization among the people with whom he worked. Their church buildings and church habits were entirely different from those practiced in Europe and in America. They came in large numbers to their houses of worship, which were architecturally "African bush" and constructed out of material that grew in abundance in the jungle. Fathers and mothers, with children carried on hips, shoulders, and heads, walked from their humble cottages to the meeting house. Some brought little stools, for there were not enough benches for all to be seated in the church. Accustomed to carrying loads as heavy as a large container of palm oil or as light as a pencil on their heads, some came in with a hymnal, and a few toted Bibles.

The church building was always packed for service. Everyone perspired profusely. There were no handkerchiefs to wipe off the perspiration. It ran and flowed over their heads and backs and dripped on the floor. The service opened with a prayer by the teacher spoken partly in Efik and partly in English. Then came a hymn. Only a few used the hymnal, but the congregation nevertheless sang enthusiastically. Most of them knew the songs by heart, and only familiar ones were used. The tunes were African, and this delighted Henry. A scripture lesson was read, another prayer spoken, another hymn sung, and then came the sermon. The sermon was delivered by the teacher in Efik, while an interpreter explained to Henry what was being preached. Most of the sermons, said Henry, were "not bad." After the sermon each member was given the opportunity to share his blessings with God. A large heavy brass plate was used to gather the gifts, for the local coin, called a manilla, was very large and heavy. Among them would be a few English coins. The service was closed with the

Efik rendition of "Praise God from Whom All Blessings Flow." Henry felt certain that the Lutheran Church would flourish in Ibibio land.

In March, 1938 Helen returned home, leaving Henry behind. Adolf Hitler and his German war machine were readying for a penetration of Poland. Rumblings of a global war that might involve the United States were felt everywhere and word had reached Helen's family that unless they took fast action it might be difficult for her to return since she had no citizenship papers. Her sons went to work on the problem and Helen re-entered the United States without any trouble. Her children were at the New York wharf to greet her. She looked fine, but the constant use of quinine in Africa had seriously impaired her hearing. It was hoped that with proper attention this infirmity would clear as she continued her life with her loved ones in North Carolina.

At the end of April 1938, Henry again stood on the same pier in Port Harcourt where he bade Helen good-bye a few weeks earlier. This time he greeted five fellow workers: William and Mrs. Schweppe, Vernon Koeper and his wife, and Helen Kluck, a nurse. After several minor difficulties, the party of Lutheran workers arrived in Nung Udoe and were safely quartered in their respective places of labor. With their coming, the second phase of the struggle for the faith in Ibibio land had begun.

William and Mrs. Schweppe and Helen Kluck moved to the new mission house at Obot Idim and began to familiarize themselves with the work in the 16 congregations in the northern part of the field. Vernon and Mrs. Koeper stayed with Henry at Nung Udoe to acquaint themselves with the work in the 16 congregations in the southern field. Schweppe was to manage the Central School and Koeper was to handle the finances. This division of labor meant that the work load in Africa had doubled in size since Henry's arrival.

Henry worked another half year until he had the assurance that the new missionaries, together with the best men of Ibesikpo, were in a position to carry on. Then he arranged for a general conference of all the churches affiliated with the Synodical Conference. The Africans bade him a tearful farewell when he took leave for his homeland.

During his stay in Nigeria, Africa, Henry was on the go before dawn until well into the night, with many interruptions of his sleep, seven days a week. He conducted meetings and instructed teachers, catechists, and others; he counseled, settled disputes, worked on translations, and administered aid to the sick and the dying. But the Lord granted him a special measure of strength, and he experienced no sickness. William H. Schweppe, who worked with him in the bush, said of him: "We venture to say that during the eighteen months he met more people, made more friends, and was permitted to bring the message of God's love in Jesus to more Africans than many who have spent a decade and more on the Dark Continent."

He was able to look back to see that the mission had been firmly established on a sound scriptural basis with a genuine Lutheran confessionalism. Schweppe was moved to say of his coworker: "May the efforts of this man serve to awaken in the hearts of all people a greater interest in the great and blessed work which the Lord has given us to do in Africa. Yes, may it help to show and convince the whole church that our one great mission in the world is missions."

After a brief stay in Germany to visit relatives and friends, the only time he saw them before the outbreak of World War II, Henry arrived in New York in the winter of 1938-1939. Two of his very best friends, Walter Schiebel, pastor of a black congregation in Washington, D.C., and Clemonce Sabourin, were on the pier to meet him. Clemonce invited him to spend the night at his home located in the heart of Harlem, where Clemonce served St. Matthew's Lutheran Church as pastor. At dinner that evening with the Clemonces and Schiebel, Henry, who had served in mission with black colleagues on two continents, impulsively expressed his inner feeling: "This is the atmosphere in which I feel perfectly at home."

Henry filled his brief period of vacation with numerous lectures on his work in Africa. He also began to put in writing some of his experiences, under the title *We Move Into the Bush*. On March 1, 1939, he reassumed his duties at Immanuel Lutheran College. In the same year, Jonathan Udoe Ekong, the man from Ibesikpo most responsible for Henry's trip to Africa, completed his studies and returned to work among his own people.

CHAPTER 18

Henry had worked incessantly during his months in Africa. But they were one of the more peaceful periods in his hectic life. Now he returned to the battlefield. Somewhat mellowed, he nevertheless felt himself beleaguered on every side. He wanted to keep the good will of the board and at the same time the confidence of the faculty. This was most difficult, if not impossible, since members of the faculty and members of the board had their set opinions about the existing problems.

Immanuel remained a stepchild of the mission among the Blacks, Henry concluded. Although the Administration Building had been completely renovated in 1932, he saw neglect everywhere and interpreted it as an "I-don't-care" spirit of the board. He referred to the auditorium as no more than a structure filled with antique chairs enshrined in 1906. Not a new chair had been added as late as the end of the thirties. The faculty houses were in desperate need of repair. The prevailing climate was best felt in a letter written by Henry to Louis A. Wisler:

> You should not be surprised at the deplorable condition. Would you please remember the evening of your visit here sometime in 1940, when Professor Pennekamp and myself wanted to talk to you about this very building (which was one of the faculty residences) and about the fact that the members of the Board left it vacant while it paid rent for three men connected with the college to live in town. You resented so strongly our attempt to speak to you that you left us standing behind my house and left in a rage. There you had the first opportunity to learn something about that house and its condition. Again you were here last spring. There was your second chance to learn something about that house, but you carefully avoided any mentioning of it. You knew it was a disagreeable subject. I am, therefore, definitely surprised that you are now surprised at the reported deplorable condition of the vacant building.

A feeling of suspicion existed also among faculty members. Professor William Kampschmidt refrained from entering any faculty home to give suggestions of repair. William Gehrke tried to be excused from completing a questionnaire about Immanuel; he felt it would not be conducive to congeniality. He succeeded in not giving the desired information; this caused Wisler to remark that he did not expect to get the information desired. And when Louis Buchheimer, Sr., a prominent Missouri Synod clergyman, resigned after 18 months of teaching at Immanuel, Henry commented, "He got his nose full and left."

For some time Henry harbored in his make-up a latent distrust of men who were in supervisory and controlling positions in the mission, especially if they were domiciled in the Midwest. His experiences with many ethnic groups and various denominational persuasions among Christians developed in him an attitude of cooperation and of acceptance that frequently clashed with the parochial mind of the midwesterner, whose everyday activity brought him in contact with Lutheran after Lutheran. The struggles that ensued throughout the years tabbed him as a "no team man." He never was able to live down this feeling of the members of the board. Looked on as an individualist, he was never taken into full confidence. In moments of crisis he was inclined to go off in his own direction, do whatever had to be done, and then report his action to appropriate authority. Yet when asked to rescind a particular statement, which he had to do quite often, he seemed always ready, after some heated exchanges, to do what his superiors asked him. Achievement of part of a goal, he figured, was better than nothing at all.

Not all of Henry's life was a continuous hassle. There were many joyful moments, especially when he had the opportunity to talk about Africa. Neither Henry nor Helen had accumulated tons of souvenirs, but visitors could not fail to note a number of interesting items that graced their home. Masks that had been worn in primitive rituals, and beautiful handmade rugs and wall mementos were visible tokens of affection their African friends had for the Naus. There were figurines and tables with hand-carved surfaces that depicted the everyday life of people in the bush. Henry appreciated the art and craft of Africans, not as objects to satisfy curiosity, but as expressions of their creators' personal identity and distinctive cultural achievements. People were Henry's obsession, and any guests who came merely to gawk soon found themselves drawn into discussions about people, especially people who had become sharers in the Great Commission.

Henry knew how to tell a story, and never ran out of episodes. At the end of a breathtaking series, he would solemnly affirm: "In the bush of Africa one expects the best but is ready for the worst." His understanding of racial issues found succinct expressions that would in time require certain modifications: "The African is a man who has not been cowed by the white man. He receives you on his own footing, and you receive him on his. He is not like the American Negro, who, because of slavery, has knuckled under to the demands and commands of the white man."

In his many conversations he expressed his deep conviction about work in Africa. He had seen the exceptional growth of Islam. He knew of no other way of stopping it than by expansion of the Christian church. The Christian church, he insisted, must build a bulwark of mission stations on the continent of Africa which would extend from the Atlantic Ocean to the Red Sea directly below the Sahara Desert. It was a colossal undertaking, the dream of a man inspired in mission. It was a dream that led Henry gradually to rethink the work of the Lutheran church in its mission enterprise throughout the world. For the dream was not one of fantasy, but of the church's great commitment to responsible adventure in history.

CHAPTER 19

Flames had engulfed the entire world by 1941. The Allies, led by the United States, England, France, and the Soviet Union, were pitted against the powers of the Axis nations — Germany, Italy, and Japan. World War II was raging. What would happen to Henry's dream concerning Africa? Would not the battles in North Africa prove a deterrent to a peaceful plan of spreading the gospel of love and brotherhood? Would not the war in general ruin every hope of building a bulwark of Christian mission stations in Africa? Would it not especially shatter his hope of returning to India?

During the awesome and destructive years of war, from 1941-45, Henry said very little, if anything at all, about the purposes, the nature, the conduct, and the results of the war. Some of the students at Immanuel called him a Nazi. Not that he propagandized for Hitler's Third Reich, but his love of all people, his pacifistic silence, his demand for obedience and discipline, and his philosophy of joy through work gave some students the feeling that he was a sympathizer of the German people. To them these traits were Teutonic and Aryan.

Nothing was more shattering to his plans than the war. He had hoped for a quick move by his church into Africa. This was now impossible. He had also aimed to reinstitute work among the Muslims in India which had been temporarily halted when missionary Adolph Brux was dismissed from service on a charge of praying with Christians of other denominations. The Lutheran Church-Missouri Synod termed such activity "unionism."

The war now called a halt also to this plan of Henry's. To top it all, his son Henry Richard answered his country's call to serve as one of her first fighter pilots. He prayed for his son's safety daily. But when he wrote to him, he put everything on a postal card.

Because of their ministerial status, Walter and John were not eligible for the draft. Eric, who had been severely injured in his accident at Mebane, North Carolina, in 1939, was declared unfit for army service.

These were indeed difficult days for Henry and Helen. Both had loved ones in Germany, and both loved the United States. But their inability to return to the mission fields of the larger world they had long known posed the greatest burden.

Yet war and personal anxieties did not prevent Henry from dreaming and planning. Nor did the heavy responsibilities of the presidency of Immanuel deter him from laying plans for the future. The war could not last forever. The fact that he was aging, year by year, never entered his mind. He must return to India, he kept repeating to himself.

The Lutheran Church-Missouri Synod had worked among Muslims in India. Henry felt the time had come to start again. All of his energies now centered around "the forgotten man," as he called the people of the world of Islam.

In the summer of 1941 the men of Ascension Lutheran Church, Charlotte, North Carolina, at the suggestion of their pastor, Leslie Frerking, invited Henry to speak on this matter. On that occasion he related the history of Islam from 622 A.D. to the present time. He emphasized that the faith of Mohammed embraced more than one-seventh of the human race. He recited the early missionary efforts of the Christian church to convert Muslims, not by love but by the sword. He recalled the heroics of Raymond Lull, who, after vain attempts to interest others to work among Muslims, went himself and at the age of eighty became the alleged first Christian martyr among the Muslims. In his address he noted at the hand of his bitter experiences in India and Africa, how the church scarcely ever worked in earnest where the need was the greatest. With all the earnestness and enthusiasm he could muster, Henry appealed to his hearers to join him in prayer and to work with him in arousing the conscience of the Lutheran church for "the forgotten man."

After his presentation, the assembled group gathered a love offering for the speaker. The outpouring of gifts was unusually generous. Contrary to the wishes of the givers, Henry refused to accept anything beyond the amount of his round trip bus fare from Greensboro to Charlotte. He reminded them that he was receiving his regular salary from the Mission Board of the Synodical Conference. In response to their insistence that he take the money, he suggested that the remaining amount become seed money for a mission fund to encourage the church to work among Muslims. The suggestion was well received, and at every subsequent meeting of these laymen in Charlotte, North Carolina, an offering was invited for Muslim missions.

Soon after his visit to Ascension in Charlotte, Henry received monetary gifts for the Muslim fund from other Lutheran churches that had heard of his efforts. Some were as far away as California. As time passed, "the forgotten man" was remembered with gifts by an ever-increasing number of people. By 1943 a tract entitled "The Forgotten Man" was published and distributed under the sponsorship of St. Stephen's Lutheran Sunday School of Hickory, North Carolina. Henry had written the tract to arouse the consciences of Christian children, asking them to pray and to give of their gifts for helping these people.

The little seed that was sown in the summer of 1941 kept on growing. In the spring of 1944 Henry addressed the student bodies of the seminaries at St. Louis, Missouri, and Springfield, Illinois. Dr. Louis J. Sieck, president of Henry's alma mater was especially interested in his plans and sympathetic toward them. Church groups invited him to bring his message. He traveled more and more, and what was once a spark in his heart now became a flame that excited many. That same year Samuel M. Zwemer, a veteran missionary to the Muslims and editor of *The Moslem World,* gave the fledgling project a helping hand. He spoke to the pastors of the Missouri Synod's Southeastern District, assembled in Washington, D.C., encouraging them to give their support to missions among the Muslims.

Henry now absorbed himself in the effort. Besides filling speaking engagements in all parts of the country, he threw himself into the study of the language, culture, and religion of the Muslim World. Even Canada invited him. Many friends were found for the cause, conspicuous among whom were W.B. Rutledge Rhyne, Rudolf Ressmeyer, Sr., Robert Landeck, Edward Engelbert, Richard Meibohm, Louis Sieck, Ernest Hahn, Robert Stade, and many, many others. The churches of the Synodical Conference were finally awakening to the urgency of this work. Henry was thrilled with every moment of his participation in the new developments. They seemed to recharge his life that had been sapped by the recurrent problems of the college.

During a district convention of the Missouri Synod, in Cedar Rapids, Iowa, Henry found himself growing restless as he listened to a dull presentation of financial reports after his own address on mission work. He turned to several friends and quietly inquired of them whether there was a chance for a bit of sightseeing. "In Cedar Rapids?" they asked. He assured them that in this mid-American town there was indeed a strange sight — a Muslim mosque. He wanted to see it, and hoped his colleagues would also be interested. Two responded in the affirmative. They were rather doubtful about the accuracy of Henry's information but were sports enough to look for the place. They left the convention and drove leisurely along the city's streets. Suddenly Henry's eyes brightened. On the exterior of a building, in the middle of the block, he saw Arabic letters that spelled out: "Allah's House of Prayer." Henry was not a bit surprised, but he had proved to his friends that in the very heart of America, even in a place where the Lutheran church was most visible by its many churches, the religion of Islam was being propagated. Muslims were building fortresses in the very back yard of Christian communities. The sightseeing tour had made more of an impact than the address he had delivered at the convention that morning.

CHAPTER 20

Prospect of work among the Muslims brought Henry immense joy. However, the situation at Immanuel was not at all encouraging. A diminishing student enrollment and a louder cry for the closed-door policy drove him into even greater dependence on the power, grace, and love of the God who had rescued his life in the dark days of 1902. Unless God blessed the house that he had hoped to build, Henry knew that he would labor in vain. Neither a host of sympathetic Christian people, nor the strongest leadership of his church, nor even his closest friends who were promoting his efforts in behalf of "the forgotten man" would be able to open the door for entry of the message of Christ to the millions of Muslims in the world who were not being reached by other Christian groups. If the project he had in mind were to succeed, God would have to intervene. Henry had never made a show of his prayer life. Family devotions were often led by Helen, for Henry was heavily occupied at the college and in travels throughout the country, yet Henry's life was an unceasing prayer, and now, like Jacob, he wrestled with his Father in prayer.

Leslie Frerking often traveled with Henry to the conventions of the Southeastern District. They rode trains. Most of the time they used day coaches, but occasionally enjoyed the comforts of a Pullman car. On one of these trips Henry's prime objective was to urge the Southeastern District to petition the Lutheran Church-Missouri Synod to begin work among the Muslims. The overriding issue of the convention, so far as Henry was concerned, was support for this request. When time came to plead the cause, he was excited and filled with great expectations. But while he was speaking, he sensed that the door he was trying to open was being shut tight. He felt he was pleading with people whose ears and hearts were closed. He was no stranger to discouragement, but this disheartenment was new to him. For three days he fought, but everywhere he turned he thought he saw the door slamming even more tightly. His effort at the convention had been a total failure, he concluded.

It was 1944. Henry was now 63 years old. On the homeward journey, Leslie and Henry shared the same Pullman compartment. As the train rattled through Virginia, the two friends engaged in quiet conversation. Leslie noticed that whenever the conversation drifted to the recent events of the convention, Henry showed a marked depression. He was convinced that Henry was berating himself over his lack of success in selling the Muslim venture to the delegates. From their conversation it was clear to Frerking that Henry did not value diplomacy as a primary virtue. At the same time, the crusty missionary ascribed his failure to deficiency in that area. Had Henry lost his ability to cope? Frerking asked himself.

Soon it was time for sleep. Henry preferred the upper berth and informed Leslie that he was ready to retire. Under this arrangement, he would occupy his sleeping quarters first without disturbing Leslie, who was to occupy the lower berth. Before bedding down, Henry went to the men's room, while Leslie browsed through some convention materials. Fifteen minutes passed, and Henry had not returned. Thirty minutes, and still no Henry. Forty minutes passed, and Frerking became alarmed. Suddenly the thought struck Leslie that the strenuous three-day effort at the convention might have taken an even heavier toll of Henry than he had first suspected. Henry bore his years well, Leslie thought, and he was strong in mind and spirit, but it was just possible that he might have suffered a stroke or a heart attack. Leslie jumped to his feet and ran to the men's room. The door was not locked, but Frerking had difficulty pushing it open. Something seemed to be blocking it. He pushed a little harder, and the narrow aperture gave him a chance to look into the rest room. To his surprise, he saw his friend on the floor, wrestling with the Lord, in deep meditation and prayer. Leslie closed the door quietly and returned to the compartment. After Henry returned, Leslie did not say a word about what he had seen and heard. He realized that Henry was deeply troubled and had turned to the Helper, who had controlled and guided his life. He now simply laid everything at God's feet. And it happened in the men's room of a Pullman car of the Southern Railway.

CHAPTER 21

To Henry's knowledge, the Lutheran Orient Missionary Society, organized by Lutherans of six different synods with headquarters in Hamilton, Ohio, was the only Lutheran organization in the United States that had made a serious attempt at work among the Muslims. Could the Lutheran Church-Missouri Synod disregard his pleas to make its contribution to the work?

The movement for the evangelistic enterprise slowly gained momentum, and Henry mounted a more intensified and organized effort. Three days after Christmas of 1944 eleven interested men met at Henry's home in Greensboro. Among them were his personal friends Leslie Frerking, Robert L. Landeck, and Richard Meibohm, who were to contribute much of their interest and love to this undertaking. Informally, they discussed the missionary policy of the Christian church since the time of the Apostles. Their remarks called attention to the ever-increasing softness and effeminate character of the Christian church as a whole in its response to the problem of evangelizing the world. Instead of working where the need was greatest, churches had developed the policy of doing mission work where the most converts could be won with the least expenditure of time, men, and money. The result was that the most difficult mission fields were relatively untouched. Among these were practically all Muslim countries.

These eleven men were honest enough to see that this same type of calculated attitude was evident in the Lutheran Church-Missouri Synod. It had always stepped into areas in India, in China, and in Africa, where other missions had performed the rough spade work. Henry and his friends therefore hoped that in response to the challenge of work among the Muslims the Missouri Synod would take the lead by proposing its services. After much talk, the eleven voted to organize the Society for the Promotion of Mohammedan Missions. The purposes of the Society were to make known the need for missions among the Mohammedans; to awaken the members of the Missouri Synod to fulfill their obligation to "the forgotten man"; and to muster a concerted effort to bring this urgent problem to the attention of the church so that it might be included in the postwar planning of the mission outreach.

Officers were elected, with Henry chosen as chairman, Robert L. Landeck as secretary, and W.B. Rutledge Rhyne treasurer. The first appointee to the executive committee was Leslie Frerking, who had also been the first to encourage Henry in the very earliest days of his efforts to stir up interest in bringing Muslims to Christ. Before adjournment, they decided that the officers were to serve until the first general meeting of the newly founded society at the time of the convention of the Southeastern District in Baltimore, Maryland, June 12-14, 1945, when permanent officers were to be elected. Charter memberships in the Society were kept open to all individuals who joined prior to July 1, 1945. The Men's Club of Ascension Lutheran Church of Charlotte was asked to serve as custodian of the Mohammedan mission fund. All contributions were deposited through the temporary treasurer.

Among the eleven who had met with Henry during the Christmas holidays of 1944 were some who felt that Henry had all the qualifications for heading up the mission department of Concordia Seminary, St. Louis, Missouri. Some even thought that Henry might himself be harboring the idea. Such a post would be a joy for this man of mission, they said among themselves. But someone asked, "Wouldn't he miss the excitement of direct involvement in mission?"

The executive committee met on February 7 and again on May 2, 1945. At those meetings it was decided that the Society publish a modest, informative pamphlet, which was to appear prior to the general meeting in June. The small publication was called *The Minaret*, the name chosen by Henry. It was sent to all members of the Society, to all the pastors of the Missouri Synod, and to every society and church that had contributed to the objectives of the organization. A tentative constitution and bylaws were prepared, and an agenda for the general meeting was adopted.

With great enthusiasm, yet with some apprehension, Henry attended the convention of the Southeastern District in the summer of 1945. At Immanuel Lutheran Church, on June 13, at one o'clock in the afternoon, the meeting opened. Henry poured out his very heart as he spoke briefly of the objectives of the organization. He urged everyone present to join this society in order to awaken the Christians of the Lutheran church to a consciousness of the need for Christian missions among the Muslims. He urged them to arouse the consciences of Lutheran Christians to a realization of their clear obligation to meet this need in obedience to the Savior's missionary command. He pointed out that one of the objectives was to acquaint the church with the problems peculiar to mission work among the Muslims by providing information about the Muslim world, the missionary endeavors being carried on at the present time, and the finding of possible fields of mission activity among the Muslims. He expressed the hope that concerned leaders of the church would awaken the consciences of Christians everywhere, especially in his own church body. Behind all of this mental and spiritual anguish undoubtedly rested the hidden hope that someday he and Helen would return to the East, perhaps even to India, which held his interest and fascination throughout his life.

During the meeting of the Society, held according to plans at the convention site, a constitution was adopted. The charter members also decided that Henry was the natural choice for editorship of *The Minaret*, a post he gladly and willingly accepted.

Henry returned to Greensboro with high hopes for the success of a venture that was no longer the dream of one man. Now he was filled with a spirit that would never die. Even members of his family were at a loss to comprehend the energy their father was putting into this effort. He spoke to Eric about a frontispiece for *The Minaret* and shared the idea he had in his mind; a mosque with a towering minaret, and in the background a raised cross lighting the area. Eric had some artistic talent and drew a picture of what Henry had in mind. Henry was satisfied, and the drawing was reproduced on the frontispiece of every edition of *The Minaret*. The minaret represented the call of the muezzin urging every faithful Muslim to face Mecca and pray. The towering cross of Christ represented the invitation of Jesus Christ to the world of Islam.

In the first publication Henry pleaded that the Society was not a church within a church but an organization designed to heighten awareness about the importance of beginning mission work in the world of Islam. He believed that participation in this work was the duty and privilege of the entire church, including Lutherans in the Missouri Synod. He desired to bring what he regarded the greatest of all missionary problems to the attention of the church in order that the church, through its existing agencies, might move into action.

Henry was convinced that the Great Commission, to proclaim the gospel in all the world, did not direct the church to reach out only to those who knew absolutely nothing of Christianity. Muslims, who had a long history of acquaintance with Christianity, were also entitled to the fullness of the gospel. The church, he said, could not claim fidelity to its missionary obligation if it shied away from work among Muslims. Nor could the Missouri Synod claim that it might be acting too hastily, he chided. Luther died in 1546. Surely 400 years had given his followers enough time to think on this and assorted other obligations. In this spirit and with the prayer that God would bless *The Minaret*, he mailed the first edition. Abraham's prayer became his prayer: "Oh that Ishmael might live before thee."

While absorbed in this venture, Henry experienced a number of changes at home and at times felt that he shared in the tribulations of Job. Six years after the death of his mother, his father wanted to return to Germany. Peter was homesick for his daughters and old-time friends in Wiesbaden, and Henry and his brothers arranged for his return to the homeland. After his departure, Eric took over the five-acre farm, lived on it, and raised his family. Henry had a special affection for Eric, and this son's accident at Mebane had been a hard blow. Eric's recovery was long and painful, but after a year he was able to lead a normal life. Since farming was something of a mutual interest, Henry came often to assist Eric. He also made Eric a gift of $2,000, a sum saved during his stay in Africa. He explained that it was in partial payment for permitting his parents to live on Eric's property rent free for so many years.

In 1942 came the news of daughter Esther's death. In the late thirties she had married Ed Runge, who at the time of her death ministered in Grafton, North Dakota. She died very suddenly, eleven days after giving birth to her first-born. Tears came to Henry's eyes when he received the news. It was one of the rare moments in his life that he showed outward grief. Henry and Helen buried her in the Forest Lawn Cemetery at the Guilford County Courthouse Battlefield, where, encouraged by their daughter Mary Ann and her husband, Ralph, they purchased a burial site.

In 1944 and again in 1946 he learned of the serious illness of his son, John, who was a pastor at that time in New Orleans, Louisiana. Henry invited him and his family to come to North Carolina to recuperate. By that time Henry and Helen were living in the smaller faculty residence on campus, long occupied by the Kampschmidt family. The president's home, which had been their domicile for almost twenty years, was now used by black faculty members.

Henry also suffered his first serious illness since the dysentery he had once contracted in India. He noticed that he was not able to urinate freely. This condition, together with the sign of blood particles in his urine, disturbed him. Having had a previous attack in 1941, he wasted no time in contacting his personal physician, whom the family remembered simply as Dr. Durham, who diagnosed the trouble as an enlarged prostate gland. Durham advised an operation and urged Henry to seek admission to the Bowman-Gray Memorial

Hospital in Winston-Salem, North Carolina. This medical center had an excellent reputation, with a competent staff of surgeons. Henry chose to have the work done there. Helen accompanied him and stayed at the home of Richard Meibohm. No one really knew what was in Henry's mind as he lay on his hospital bed that October, 1945. Only what he confided to Helen bared his inner feeling. He questioned his chances of ever getting back to India now that he was a sick man. But he shared none of his anxieties with his sons and daughters. He gave them the impression that he possessed a never-say-die spirit.

The operation was successful. He returned to Greensboro and Immanuel. At the hospital he had been a pleasant patient; at home he was irritable. He could not endure idleness, nor did he think he was very sick. But his recovery was slow. During his absence from class, Clemonce Sabourin, pastor of Grace Lutheran, occupied his teaching chair. However, Henry was determined to lose no more days than necessary. In typical Henry Nau fashion, impulsive and hasty, he entered his classrooms and taught from a wheelchair. Gradually, despite his disregard of doctor's orders, he regained his full strength and assumed all his responsibilities. He was now in his sixty-fifth year.

By this time he could well have retired to the ranks of senior citizens, but his enthusiasm, willingness to work, and philosophy of missions kept him moving full steam ahead. A man with such a spirit created confidence in many colleagues, both young and old. After many years of isolation from white workers because of his labors among Blacks, he now received the respect and love of white pastors, teachers, and people, particularly in the southeastern part of the United States.

The love of brother ministers surfaced, especially at a banquet in Washington, D.C., to which Henry and Helen had been invited. To his great surprise, he was called to the rostrum by the master of ceremonies. Asked to bring his faithful and loving wife with him, he cautiously approached the speakers' table. Leslie Frerking stood up to address the assembly. He expressed the admiration and love that all the fellow workers in the ministry had for Henry and Helen and presented to them a rather large package. Henry was asked to unwrap the package in the presence of the assembled audience.

Tears flooded his eyes as he looked on a gift that he would never have guessed in a hundred years. He was not in the habit of parading his intelligence, but ever since 1920, when he received his Doctor of Philosophy degree, his status as an educated person had been affirmed by the endearing name of "Doc." Now before his eyes there was, of all things, a doctor's gown. Frerking requested Helen to help him put it on. Now dressed in the full grandeur of a brand new doctor's gown, the first and only one he owned in his life, he expressed his most heartfelt thanks. He then turned to Helen and softly but audibly said to her, "Mama, now I am somebody." He used the gown at several commencement occasions, but gave it to his oldest son, Walter, when the latter received his Doctor of Philosophy degree from Duke University, at Durham, North Carolina. Henry felt more at ease in an inexpensive business suit; in fact, he paid so little attention to what he wore that he left all such matters to Helen, who bought every piece of his apparel.

CHAPTER 22

The Society for the Promotion of Missions among the Muslims was hard at work. Even Immanuel Lutheran College was receiving more attention. The Southeastern District petitioned the representatives of the mother church to operate the school under a local board of control. This showed that many more people in the southeastern area of the country were taking an interest in the school and in the mission among the Blacks.

Both 1944 and 1945 brought unexpected problems. The war had decreased enrollment. Financial difficulties stared the school in the face like death itself. Nothing seemed to offer a ray of light, and Henry experienced a rare loss of courage.

In 1944 the members of the Mission Board of the Synodical Conference of the Lutheran Church assembled in Cleveland, Ohio. They complained that an increasing number of Negro pastors were unworthy of the office of the ministry and expressed dissatisfaction over a number of the other matters. Instead of dealing with the problems in a brotherly manner, the members of the board came out with a policy of procedures that spelled one thing clearly — Board Authority. All rights, powers, privileges, and duties incidental to, granted by, and imposed upon the corporation by the laws of the state of Missouri were to be exercised. It would issue calls to missionaries, teachers, and assistants. It reserved to itself all rights to fix salaries, to give instructions, to exercise the rights of visitation, and to dismiss workers if found unfit or unworthy of their positions.

The battle lines in 1944 between the Negro workers and the members of the Synodical Board were thus unmistakably drawn at the very time that Blacks were struggling for equality. The board defended its strong action on the ground that cases of discipline among the Negro workers had multiplied and the number of resignations had increased. Misunderstandings on the part of some superintendents in the field contributed to escalation of hostilities.

Understandably, Blacks, who had a right to expect division of responsibilities, were filled with indignation and resentment. Sixty-five years of preaching and teaching the gospel had not left them ignorant of their duties and responsibilities as defined in the Scriptures. White bureaucrats might look on many of them as children who were incapable of accepting responsibility. But, as Henry tried to point out, even children never learn to walk unless given the opportunity to do so. "The child must get on the floor, scramble around, try again and again until it succeeds and toddles alone," he would say. This was not paternalistic rhetoric on his part, but therapeutic syntax designed to heal white thinking. It seemed a losing battle. Again and again the purposes of the college were being questioned. Although many throughout the church felt that the objectives of the college in the training of ministers had been realized in spite of the open-door policy, it was resolved at Cleveland, in 1944, to close Immanuel.

This was Henry's gravest hour. The student body had been reduced drastically, and the theological department included only two students, after a high of fifteen. It seemed that the proponents of the closed-door policy had won the war. But Henry refused to admit defeat. He was dismayed when he faced the fact that the chief purpose of the institution, to train young men for ministry among Blacks, had failed. Yet he worked on. He found new inspiration in total commitment to the mission outreach. He was encouraged by others who believed that the closing of Immanuel was a fatal blow to work among the Negroes in the entire South.

In 1946 the sick body of Henry's beloved Immanuel, almost a corpse after the resolution of 1944 to close it, began to rally. Support came from friends in the Southeastern District. To his immense relief, Henry received word that a resolution, signed by Edgar C. Rakow, the secretary of the Southeastern District, had been sent to the Synodical Conference in Milwaukee urging placement of the spiritual care of "the colored (sic!) people" into the hands of the districts in which these people were located. At the same time, the general conference of the Negro churches assembled in New Orleans on July 26, 1946, came out strongly in support of Immanuel. Members of the conference expressed the feeling that it was not Immanuel's fault that pastors and teachers who had once been active in the mission had left their work, and they urged that the school be kept open under the control of a local board. The action of Cleveland to close Immanuel thus seemed to supply the spark necessary to revitalize the institution. Late in the summer of 1946 the Synodical Conference agreed to keep Immanuel open and to operate it under a local board of control.

Another blessing came from an unexpected quarter. During World War II the United States government rented seven acres of Immanuel Lutheran College to construct barracks for the Overseas Replacement Depot. For three years a wire fence divided the campus into two parts. The one part consisted of the buildings of the college; the other part contained the wooden barracks of the Overseas Replacement Depot. In the summer of 1946 this government camp was declared surplus property. The military buildings erected on the college campus, which were five in number, were given to the college by the government. They were renovated and used as a dining room, a student center, and housing for married and unmarried veterans. One of the buildings was converted into a garage storeroom and a work room, which were used for vocational training. In addition to the buildings, the college received equipment for dormitories, classrooms, and the dining room. The donated property had a value of thousands of dollars in the open market. This acquisition created a spirit of growth that assisted in keeping the institution open. The campus was beautified and many sidewalks were built. 1946 appeared like a comet in the sky for Immanuel. Optimism and hope came alive in Henry and his associates.

In the following years, many people who were interested in the college expressed the hope that the future of Immanuel would be settled in its favor. The uncertainties of the past ought to be removed, they felt. Sensing the change, Henry expressed himself in the biennial report of 1946-48:

> May I venture to say a word or two about the more promising outlook now as compared to 1946. To anyone who knew conditions in our mission and in Negro America, 1946 was the end of a dark period. I shall not touch anymore upon the causes. We can now much more confidently encourage young men to make the ministry their calling and our young men see that the Negro is given the same chance, status, respect, and compensation as his white brother. Thus the impression they have had for many years that the

Lutheran church is a white man's church where the Negro is only tolerated is gradually vanishing from our people. They begin to see their own people in responsible positions, trusted by their brethren and respected by them. Furthermore, 1946 brought the end of the war. Seminary and college students who had the ministry in view when they came here did not make use of the exemption from military service which they could have had. They did not want to bring down upon their people the evil reputation that they were shirking their duty. This emptied Negro seminaries to a large extent. Not only did our seminary suffer but many other Negro seminaries. Whitfield Theological Seminary, the Zion Methodist Episcopal Church in Salisbury, the Presbyterian Theological Seminary connected with Johnson C. Smith College in Charlotte dwindled down to just a few students. Those supporting these seminaries did not on this account contemplate closing the institutions. They knew better, and the last two years have shown that they were more right than we who wish to close this school.

Henry rejoiced to report that in February, 1948, a committee of the State Department of Education and of the Southern Association of Colleges and Secondary Schools evaluated Immanuel. The work of the committee was done in a fair and helpful spirit. What was good was freely acknowledged; what was not good was pointed out in a helpful, charitable spirit. The committee praised Immanuel as one of the very few schools in the state that lived up to its philosophy of education. The instruction given at Immanuel was termed superior. The fact that the religious element permeated not only the classroom instruction but extracurricular activities as well, thereby improving student-faculty relations and campus deportment, was highly commended. The physical equipment passed inspection. The library and the Home Economics Department received commendation. All these credits seemed to be a vindication of Henry's struggle to keep Immanuel open in commitment to mission. What was deplored were the totally inadequate salaries of the professors and instructors. Commenting on this, Henry said, "We know ourselves and our shortcomings only too well, but many are of such a nature that only the Synodical Conference can remedy them."

What Henry had endured during the turbulent years when Wisler and Wilson were executive directors was forgotten. Karl Kurth became the new executive director of the Synodical Conference in 1948. He brought a new spirit. By 1949 Henry was satisfied with the membership of the local board, not only because of the quality of its men but also because it included both whites and Blacks. In fact, two of the members of the local board, Moses Dickinson and John T. Skinner, had been students under Henry.

Henry now seemed to be consumed by two conflicting interests. One was Immanuel and the work among the Blacks in the Southeast; the other was to bring the good news to the Muslims of the world. Behind all this was the prayer and the hope that he might return to India, to the land and the people of his first love. But, despite his excellent health, advancing age threatened to be a deterrent.

CHAPTER 23

The Society for the Promotion of Mohammedan Missions was on the march. As news went through *The Minaret,* which carried many an article by Henry, monies were coming in from congregations and societies throughout the United States and Canada. Henry was booked for speeches in many states, especially those of the Midwest and North Midwest. Wherever he went, he encouraged Christians to come to the support of the work he espoused — bringing Christ to "the forgotten man." Although the Lutheran Church-Missouri Synod had not yet made any attempt to take over the work, the Society itself neither was able nor desired to go it alone. Its policy was that the synod at large should do the work while the Society worked on promotion. An informed constituency would generate the necessary financial support.

Nineteen hundred and forty-seven was a vintage year for Henry. Greater support for the institution at Greensboro was coming from various sources, and progress in race relations between members of the Board and the workers in the field was being made. This year also saw the Lutheran Church-Missouri Synod meet in convention at Chicago, Illinois. The delegates on recommendation of two of their districts, Southeastern and Eastern, and the Society for Promotion of Mohammedan Missions, voted to instruct the Foreign Mission Board, under the guidance of its executive secretary, Otto H. Schmidt, to begin an investigation for a suitable mission field among the Muslims. Henry had been praying and waiting for this action for a long time. The Society had, in fact, been organized with this as one of its objectives. The gloom was gone, and for the first time he felt that his church had come to grips with a mission endeavor that would really test its mettle.

After the decision of the Synod, a number of meetings between Schmidt and representatives of the Society for the Promotion of Christian Missions among the Mohammedans followed. Over a three-year period, 1947-1949, Henry attended as many of these meetings as he could without jeopardizing his personal contact with the paying constituency. Each speaking tour brought in additional financial support for the Society's work. At last, on February 1, 1949, in Baltimore, Maryland, the decision was reached to go ahead with the proposed mission among Muslims. The Society offered its financial support to train prospective missionaries for this exacting work. It also resolved that Henry was to spearhead the work in association with two young missionaries.

At first Henry asked himself whether this assignment meant that he would have the opportunity once more to visit India. However, the more engrossed he became in the project, the less he cared about his own geographical interests. The Muslim challenge was worldwide. Besides, it was only an exploratory trip, which would take at best only a few months, and soon he would be back in the States and at his post in Immanuel.

Where should his church go? Many countries had been mentioned as possible areas. Africa was certainly in the running. It was inhabited by millions of Muslims, and Henry had once dreamed, during his stay among the Ibesikpo people, of erecting a chain of Christian missions across the very heart of the Black Continent. The Middle East, with its many Arab nations, was another prospective area. India was always in the background as a possible field, for the Missouri Synod had worked among its Muslims from 1923 until 1936. Even the island of Java was a possibility. The only way a decision could be made was to arrange an exploratory journey to gain an on-the-spot insight. The Foreign Mission Board, together with members of the Society, came to the conclusion that the Middle East, including Iran, Iraq, Lebanon, and Jordan, was to be the target.

The Foreign Mission Board endorsed the Society's decision to send Henry on the exploratory trip to the Middle East. He was the logical choice, for he knew more about Muslim culture, religion, and life than anyone in the Missouri Synod. He had applied himself, off and on, to the study of Islam since his early years in India and had intensified his study after his venture in Nigeria. After agreeing to accept employment for a period extending from June 1, 1949 to September 1, 1950, he resigned his presidency of Immanuel but retained his position as professor, to which post he would return after his survey.

Before his departure, which was scheduled for August 17, 1949, he made provisions for Helen who was not to accompany him on this trip. He asked the board to furnish an apartment for her, but this move proved unnecessary, for shortly after his good-bye, Helen moved into a modest house for which she and Henry had contracted construction in the early summer of 1949. The Immanuel campus, which had been their home for almost 25 years, was forsaken for the house on 124 West Green Court in the western section of Greensboro.

Despite the thrill of going East to explore mission possibilities among the Muslims, Henry was still interested in Immanuel's well-being. The institution had been planning to offer the Bachelor of Divinity Degree for its theological students. This development now appeared to be in jeopardy. Without hesitation, he announced that he would forego the trip to the Middle East rather than see the degree program undermined. Only after repeated assurances that the program would not be scuttled did he complete his travel preparations and once more join the forces of his church that were active in mission throughout the world. Twenty-nine years had passed since he had been associated with the Foreign Mission Board of the Missouri Synod. Now he was eager once more to get into its action. On the eve of his departure, he said, "In one hour I leave the good U.S.A. I am deeply sensitive of the great responsibility resting upon me, and altogether I am dependent on the presence of our living Lord. If I was not sure His presence was . . . going to carry me up there, I would not want to go."

By October he was in Iran and enjoyed the hospitality of Presbyterians with whom he conferred. On his journey he kept a daily diary. He discovered that the missionary zeal of the Christian churches active among the Muslims was at a very low ebb. He found that many Iranian evangelical Christians did not believe that Muslims worshiped a different god from the one of their own faith. Not too clear on the difference between names for God and words for God, he met with strong opposition from Arab, Syrian, and Armenian Christians whenever he told them that the Allah of the Koran was not the Allah of the Arabic Bible nor the Jehovah of the Old Testament. He created a sensation in the Jordan meeting of the United Church in Jerusalem when he said that the Mohammedan god was nothing but an idol. In his inimitable manner he argued with them. He exclaimed, "If the Muslim worships the same god as I, why bring Him to that particular Muslim? Here is missing the real incentive to mission work."

Wherever he went, whether in Syria, in Iran, in Iraq, in Jordan, or in Lebanon, he found fear among the Christians and opposition to the work of the Christian church by the various governments. He noted that the Jordan government had taken 18 Muslim boys out of a Christian orphanage in Ramalla, north of Jerusalem, because they were exposed to biblical instruction. During his visit he realized that all Arab nations were fighting for their cultural unity, and their unity was in Islam. Wherever and whenever he asked the question of how much work was being done among the Muslims, he received the answer, "Very little. Hardly any." He found that only Lebanon was open to Christian teaching without government interference. In Syria he was told by a Danish Lutheran instructor that he was forbidden to teach religion in his school because almost everyone was a Muslim. The only place he was allowed to teach his faith was in his own house. No Christian chaplain was allowed to approach a Muslim patient with the gospel. Even social welfare was frequently interpreted as a cover for religious propaganda. Not a single government in this part of the world encouraged Henry to begin work among the Muslims. For the most part, even Christians in the area displayed no enthusiasm for Henry's program.

In obedience to his board's direction to explore the possibility of mission among Indian Muslims should work in the countries of the Middle East not prove feasible, Henry left for India in December, 1949. After more than 35 years, he was back in the land of his first love. In Krishnagiri he stayed with Michael Naumann, whom he had known as a little boy 44 years ago. Henry was jubilant. He wrote:

> I cannot tell you what a joy and satisfaction it is for me to be able to see again the old mission stations and meet Indian friends of forty-five years ago. In Krishnagiri yesterday together with Brother Michael I went through the bazaar street and met some merchants who still remembered me. Also in Parih-cheri I met some women now fifty years old and more whom I taught in school.

On Christmas Day, 1949, while attending a service, he was happily surprised that he could still speak Tamil. His German accent was unmistakable, and his vocabulary was somewhat limited, but he was confident that in a short time he would be speaking the language fluently. Not many days later Henry was asked to preach in one of the regular Sunday services. After presenting his message in Tamil, a colleague asked him how he managed to communicate so well after more than 35 years. Henry replied: "I never let a day pass without reading a page of the Bible in both Tamil and Malayalam."

At a conference attended by Henry in the company of Otto H. Schmidt and fellow Lutheran missionaries, the decision was made to begin work among the Muslims living on the Malabar Coast. Hope was also expressed for reopening the work in Vaniyambadi. Since Henry was now in that very area, he proceeded, immediately after Schmidt's departure for the United States, to lay the groundwork for reopening of the mission.

Implementation of the main mission endeavor took place on April 17, 1950. Henry Otten and John Gall received calls as missionaries to the Muslims and were preparing for their work at the Kennedy School of Eastern languages in Connecticut. On May 4 Henry met the young men at Madras, and work was begun at Feroke and Calicut. Despite great difficulties, Henry on his part now veritably plunged into the work. He had the enthusiasm of his young associates. Progress was slow, but from his own point of view "satisfactory," whatever that meant from a missiologist's standpoint. A reading room was opened, and by July, Henry made plans for his return to the United States. He hated to leave, but he had contracted to work only a year, and Helen was waiting for him in their new home in Greensboro.

CHAPTER 24

Nau arrived home in August, 1950. Sixty-nine years were behind him, years of hard work and dangerous living, but he bore them well. His physical and mental conditions were excellent and his spirit unflagging. Few men of his age enjoyed such blessings.

Meanwhile, Henry Otten and John Gall were hard at work in India to establish the infant mission effort among the Muslims. But all was not well. Gall, who had gone to India without his wife, began to experience marital problems. His wife was unwilling to leave the United States to join him, and attempts made in the United States to persuade her were in vain. Gall was almost a nervous wreck and little help in the exacting effort required in India. To save his personal health, his marriage, and his later usefulness in the Muslim work, he was ordered by the Missouri Synod's Foreign Mission Board to return to the United States. Suddenly it became imperative to find an experienced man to take Gall's place. God again fingered Henry. In February, 1951, the Foreign Mission Board called him as missionary to the Muslims in India.

Whatever Henry might have been thinking was reflected in his everyday activities to prepare himself and Helen for their return to the land and people they both dearly loved. A news reporter of the local paper was perplexed that a 70-year-old man could be so excited about leaving the comforts and conveniences of life in America for primitive conditions that prevailed in parts of India. "Won't that be a hardship for a man of your age? Why are you so anxious to go?" Henry replied, "Forty years ago I met a man in India who tried to persuade me to become a Muslim. I now must return to persuade him to become a Christian. I know that is God's will in my life."

In his acceptance of the call, he wrote Otto H. Schmidt and Herman H. Koppelmann that he experienced little opposition to his acceptance, particularly on the part of members of his family. But euphoria was here presiding over truth. The members of his family, particularly his sons, were not at all happy over his plans to return to India. They did not think much of his intention to take their mother, at the age of 66 years, into a land that offered in places very few, if any, comforts.

Walter, Eric, and John determined to visit their father and attempt to persuade him to reconsider his decision. Knowing that their father would never remain idle, they decided to suggest that he spend his remaining years in relaxed teaching at Immanuel. Henry, ignorant of the details, was of course delighted to learn of the interest his sons had in his work and in the welfare of their mother and he agreed to a family discussion.

A meeting of the Nau clan was a rare experience, for all of the members lived in different parts of the country. But plans finally solidified and the meeting took place. The occasion, which was the first of its kind in the new home on West Green Court, could have been a most joyful one. Everyone was happy to be at home. Mary Ann and Irene had joined their brothers. Henry Richard, who was living in Omaha, Nebraska, at the time, was the only absentee. After the evening meal, the boys supplied a case of beer and the family gathered in congenial conversation.

At last Walter approached the real purpose of their presence in Greensboro. With all the eloquence at his command, he tried to show his father the absolute foolhardiness of two aged people going to work in India. The battle lines were now drawn. Gone was the merriment. Eric and John, and at times Mary Ann and Irene, tried to reinforce Walter's argument with pleading dissuasion. But father Nau's resistance was mounting and the mood of the conversation began to change. Even the beer lost its flavor when they heard their father say, "I would rather die in India than in any other part of the world."

Such a wish shocked everyone. They all recalled that Henry had often said that the Piedmont area of North Carolina was the finest area of the world and boasted the most salubrious climate. John almost reached the point of calling his father a "crazy" man. But, respectful son that he was, he could not go that far even though he thought it. Back and forth the conversation went, with arguments pro and con.

As the hours passed, the boys were convinced that their father had a closed mind about the whole matter and gave up on him. Mother, however, was another matter! The discussion now centered on whether their father should take Helen, in her advanced age, to India. Every one of the children was dead set against her going. Realizing, however, the dedication of their mother and the desire of their father to have her with him, the boys gradually backed off from their strong feeling. No one gave consent, and there was no general agreement. Finally, Henry asked his sons to come into his study. In the center of the study stood a wooden box, large enough to hold those articles thought by Henry to be necessities for their life in India. The box was sturdily built and was already half packed. Henry stood at one end of the box while the boys faced him at the other end. He then calmly pointed to the box and said nothing. After a period of dead silence, John turned to his brothers and said, "Fellows, you have the answer. You'll never change his mind. Mama, who has been his constant companion, is going with him. I am going back to my work in South Carolina." That just about wrapped up the feeling of the family.

When Henry received the call to India, he learned something about himself. He had always looked upon members of boards as groups of men who had very little, if any, feeling for the work he did and for him as a person. Now he read words written by the Foreign Mission Board which caused him to rethink:

The Lord gave you a deep interest, fervor, and zeal for this particular kind of Christian missionary work and has equipped you with many talents and has blessed you with a ruggedness of body and courage to face difficult situations. Your experience is absolutely invaluable for this work. Your ability in cooperative efforts with national fellow workers as well as the Church in the United States is regarded as a great asset in doing this rather difficult task.

They did refer to his advanced age, which would ordinarily have disqualified a person for overseas duty, but regarded his experience and zeal as values that outweighed any other consideration. He was touched. Despite his individuality, his impatience, and his temper, he had many friends serving on the boards of the church. Filled with gratitude, he referred to them as competent men, devoted to duty, efficient, and very conscientious in their work. It seemed that the day of Missouri's Mutual Admiration Society had arrived. The executive director, Otto H. Schmidt, reciprocated by noting the good example Henry had for many years given to the younger men in the work of the church and mission.

Henry's assignment carried the instruction that the missionaries to the Muslims in India were to attend the general conference and also one district conference in their adjacent field. He was to regard the Mohammedan mission as a venture separate from the mission among the Hindus. In addition to his fixed salary, he was to receive free housing, medical care beyond the first $25 per year, expenses for official travel, six weeks of hill leave, free use of the facilities at Kodaikanal, and the payment of a part of the Missouri Synod's pension fund. He was pleased with these contractual arrangements.

Henry and Helen, with the good wishes of their otherwise disappointed children, left Greensboro on June 20, 1951. The commissioning service was held in Baltimore, Maryland, at Saint Martini Lutheran Church.

CHAPTER 25

The Naus booked passage on the *Steel Advocate,* a freighter, scheduled to make numerous port calls in countries of the Middle East. This called for visas, even though Henry and Helen were not scheduled to leave the ship at any of these foreign ports. Waiting for the visas consumed more time than expected, and Henry became uneasy. Then, with the visas secured, the longshoremen went on strike, and the *Steel Advocate* lost a week in port.

While waiting for departure, Henry wrote the members of his Foreign Mission Board for permission to purchase a refrigerator. He wanted to buy it in India and not in the United States. Despite the reasonableness of his request, he was aware that possession of a refrigerator might be considered a luxury in India, and he had always been, if anything, overly cautious about the way in which he spent monies entrusted to him. Apologetically, he stated that the board members were not to think that he was trying to get something out of the church for nothing. He added that he and Helen were ready to live in India without a refrigerator just as they had done 40 years ago when refrigerators were not available. The board granted his request.

Finally, on July 16, 1951, Henry and Helen left for the land they had called home many years ago. After 38 days on board ship, they arrived safely and with great expectation. The trip from Baltimore to Madras had been most instructive and enjoyable. On their arrival Henry was unable to locate two pieces of baggage, but he was not unduly excited. An experienced world traveler, he was confident that the baggage would be on another boat. In the customs office they were met by John Naumann, who assisted them in securing their entry permit and clearing the baggage in 30 minutes instead of the customary several hours. After attending to some personal business, they left for Vaniyambadi and arrived safely on August 9. For the first ten days they stayed with missionaries in Vaniyambadi and then occupied a small bungalow on a hillside, which gave them a beautiful view of the heavily populated low countries. Some screens in the bungalow had to be repaired and others replaced, and several pieces of furniture had to be constructed in order to make the place livable. Otherwise their living quarters were fairly comfortable.

Henry put "his hands to the plow" with enthusiasm and energy. His arrival encouraged a noticeable spirit of renewed activity among the Lutheran missionaries. Since the men working among the Hindus were not to busy themselves with work among the Muslims, the entire mission effort among the latter was on the shoulders of the two Henrys, Otten and Nau. Working from early morning to late at night, they furnished a reading room with whatever Christian literature was available in the Tamil and Malayalam languages.

Not long after his arrival Henry received $154 from friends in the States, to be spent as he saw fit. Henry used it to paint the reading room and to buy some benches and chairs. He was also now able to make several smaller rooms above the reading room available for private conference and instruction, with electric current.

The people who frequented the reading room were 75 percent Hindus and 25 percent Muslims. Henry was delighted to see Muslim high school boys and college students coming in steadily increasing numbers to inspect the literature. Muslim women came to see the missionaries but preferred coming to the house instead of the reading room. Henry engaged all of them in long conversations. After listening to Henry, those who had brought their lunch ate on the porch of the second bungalow, which at that time was vacant. At times entire Muslim high school classes came to visit the reading room for discussions with Henry. He also accepted invitations to speak to various groups, even to people associated with the Bible College located in Wandoor. He had every hope that the gospel would triumph. He realized he had a long way to go, but he had patience and trust in the Lord's power, goodness, and presence that progress would be made.

Every day he was visited by a language teacher who instructed him not only in the languages in which Henry had already developed various degrees of competence, but also in Urdu, a most difficult language to master. During his hours of language study Henry was grateful for the opportunities he had had in the past to develop his understanding of Sanskrit. He found it easier to understand the language instructor and was able to master his lessons more quickly. Still he had to struggle every day for at least six hours with Urdu. These six hours were split into three different periods: the first from 6:30 A.M. to 8 A.M.; the second from 1 to 3 P.M.; and the third from 5:30 to 8 P.M. Henry chafed under what he considered a lamentable handicap, namely, that his instructor spoke only Urdu and Telugu. If the teacher had known either English or Tamil, he would have had an easier time. But there was no escaping the task. More than 75,000 Muslims spoke Urdu in Vaniyambadi, Krishnagiri, Jegadevi, and other places in Henry's sphere of work.

Between his language lessons Henry worked on the production of literature for general distribution. Adolph Brux, one of Henry's predecessors in India, had left a number of manuscripts that he had written in Urdu. Henry reworked some of these and printed them on a press plate he had located. These, together with reprints of other articles, kept the reading room supplied.

Every Friday afternoon, from 3 to 5, he gave elementary instruction in Islamic culture and language to young Christian catechists. Experience had taught him what every missiologist considered basic, that success in mission depended in large measure on the collegial approach taken to potential local leadership. Many of the catechists had Muslim acquaintances and used their relationship as opportunity to bear witness to their faith.

Except for a few days spent at conferences of fellow Christians, Henry was "on the go." Every Wednesday, through 1951 and 1952, he made a trip to Krishnagiri to meet a Muslim, Abdur Rajak, who Henry said was "not far from the kingdom." He was a native dispenser of medicine and wanted to call his place the House of Health of the Messiah. Henry gave the man some encouragement in his work and helped him integrate his efforts with the larger mission thrust.

By February, 1952, Henry reported that missionary Otten and his wife had set up a clinic in Wandoor, located not too far from Calicut, on the far west coast of India. An Indian doctor had been engaged to operate the clinic. She was assisted by a pharmacist and several attendants. The clinic was housed in an excellent brick building, well arranged and located at the edge of town. On the average, 115 patients received service at the clinic daily.

Overwhelmed by the tremendous challenge, but without additional professional resources coming from the United States, Henry and his associate Otten themselves contacted and conversed with many Muslims about Jesus Christ. Henry did not at all object to doing this personal type of witnessing. He thrived on it, and despite his 70 years threw himself into the task, without regard to personal health and well-being. But he was chagrined that his church appeared to be dragging its feet in getting additional people to work among the Muslims in India.

Henry wanted things to happen yesterday and he was sharply critical, both of the sending church for not sending more person power and of young seminarians for showing so little interest in foreign service. He took a dim view of seminary graduates who were more interested in securing advanced degrees at other divinity schools than in "sinking their teeth into the real work," living among Muslims, and telling them about the saving work and Lordship of Jesus Christ.

His interest in acquiring more people to work directed his attention to other areas of the church. He suggested that if Americans were not available, the Free Church of Germany should be asked to help. In the closing days of 1951 and the early days of 1952 the Board of Foreign Missions assured Henry that firm efforts were being made to secure more men for the field. His enthusiasm was contagious and began to bridge continents and oceans. Fresh interest stirred in the United States at both seminaries of the Missouri Synod. Especially members of the Synod in the Midwest area, where Lutheranism was strongest in number, were learning more about the work among "the forgotten man."

Finally, in the late spring of 1952, Henry received the best news he had heard for some time. Roland Miller had received a scholarship from the Society for the Promotion of Mohammedan Missions to study for a year at the Kennedy School of Missions in Connecticut. Another candidate, Ernest Hahn, had taken the courses in the St. Louis-based School of Mission and he and his wife Greta were to sail for India on December 17 of the same year.

Before the arrival of Hahn, Henry had called for at least one additional man. He let his board know that there was room for one more on the compound where he lived; in fact, two more men, he wrote, could room with him and Helen, since they were not using the upstairs bedroom nor the second bedroom downstairs. Separate bath facilities were available. In addition, one big bungalow at the site was entirely empty.

Still desperate for workers, Henry tried to tap the church's supply of ministerial veterans. The "old men at home" really did not know what they missed in not coming to the foreign field, he wrote. "This is a grand life, brethren; not a dull moment even in writing this letter!" Lest his board think that the Indian heat had gotten to him, Henry assured them that Muslim women were not afraid to remove their veils before an old man like him. Couldn't they send a man about sixty years old to help? While awaiting a response to his plea, he sang a "Te Deum" when he learned of the possibility of expanding the clinic at Wandoor into a full hospital.

In his description of the grand life, Henry thought primarily of the great opportunities offered for bearing witness to faith. He was almost unaware of the everyday trials of the life of a missionary in India, even in the latter half of the 20th century. Helen was far less myopic. Standards of living in India had improved a thousandfold since the beginning of the century, when both she and her loved one engaged in their first labors among the Indians, but indigenous hazards had not disappeared, she said. The cobra was still as prevalent as always, she wrote. During the dry season one had to walk most circumspectly. This was the time when the cobra gave birth and could be most vicious in her attack on anyone who ventured near her brood. Helen warned anyone who came to visit them on the hill to remain on the main pathway. It was most dangerous to wander off into unknown territory.

From the second floor of his bungalow, on a hill-site vantage point, Henry could see five mosques in Vaniyambadi. The view rekindled his anticipation of a permit to address Muslim congregations in Krishnagiri, 35 miles away. He looked for every opportunity to bring the message. Throughout his feverish activity he continued to enjoy the best of health. Yet occasionally he mentioned that he experienced pains in his shoulders and arms.

CHAPTER 26

Much of Nau's time in Vaniyambadi was spent in speaking with people whom he met in the marketplace. The majority of the inhabitants went early to their fields to plow and plant grain. But instead of spending most of his time there, Henry made the rounds of the marketplaces where he was certain to find a group gathered, made up mostly of men, for the women were in the fields.

The mission had made an Austin car available to Henry. Just as the sun was rising over the Yellagiri Hills, which overlooked Vaniyambadi, he would pick up his coworkers and be on the way. The road to the marketplace in his immediate area was wide and partly blacktopped, flanked on both sides with tamarind and banyan trees. After traveling about eight miles, they turned off from the main road and stopped at a small village, where the newly built road came to an end. On the advice of an elderly Muslim woman, who was not afraid to show her face and speak with them, they parked their car there under a tamarind tree. Henry and his colleagues divided into two groups. Henry's group walked through small grain fields and rejoiced that this year the fields were green with grain and that the people, after four years of drought, would get a full harvest. They crossed a narrow irrigation lake which was filled to overflowing and contributed to the newly found prosperity. Henry observed that the people would have "a full stomach."

Just past the lake, they reached a small temple where Hanuman, the monkey god, was standing in stone with a garland around his neck. The scene reminded him of an earlier encounter with this Indian god in days when he possessed less wisdom. Near the village, they saw a few women winnowing grain on the large open space in front of the temple. On seeing them, one of the women asked, "What do you want here so early this morning?"

Henry replied, "If you want to know, come along; we will tell you."

"What will you tell us?"

"What no one has ever told you before."

"So? What may that be?"

"Come and hear."

They left their rice and winnowing fans and followed at a distance. Arriving at the village proper, one of the men who had brought along a drum began to beat it while singing a Christian lyric. As they moved in that manner through the village, a number of men, women, and children followed until they reached the center of the village. Henry found a long bench in front of a house with over-hanging eaves. It was made of sun-dried dirt but was sturdy enough to hold him and a middle-aged man of the village. The middle-aged fellow noticed that someone had sat down next to him and he stretched out his right arm to touch Henry. Since Henry was wearing pants instead of the customary loin cloth, the man asked, "Where do you come from?"

"From Vaniyambadi."

"From Vaniyambadi? What part?"

"Outside of Vaniyambadi, about one mile from Pudur. There is a wooded hill on which three bungalows are built. I live in one of them."

"Oh. Those are the padrae bungalows. Are you a padrae?"

"Yes. I am one," replied Henry.

After their exchange of introductions the conversation, as Henry recounted it later in his Teutonic English, went as follows:

"Well, if you are a padrae, perhaps you can help me to get back my eyes."

"What? Are you blind?"

"Yes, I am."

"Have you always been blind?"

"No. There was a time when I could see, but several years have passed that I can't see."

"Nothing at all?"

"No, nothing at all."

"And now you want your sight back?"

"Yes, I wish I could have it back."

"What for do you want your sight back?"

"Oh, I would like to see."

"What would you like to see?"

"Oh, everything round about here."

"Why? Have you never seen the things round about you?"

"Yes, I have seen them all and know how they look."

"And yet you want to see them again?"

"Yes."

"You have seen your house?" asked Henry.

"Yes, I know how it looks, the outside and the inside."

"What else would you like to see?"

"My wife and my children."

"You know how they look, do you?"

"Yes, I know how they look."

"You know whether your wife has black or white hair, or hair that is something between white and black?"

"Yes, yes, she had black hair when I saw her last time; but by this time there may be some white between."

"And what else would you like to see?"

"Oh, the sheep and the goats and the cows round about here."

"You have seen them before and you know how they look."

"Yes, I have seen them before many times and know how the sheep and the goats and the cows look."

"And what else are you so anxious to see?"

"My neighbors."

"Them, too, you have seen before and you can even now speak to them."

"Yes, all that I know."

"And what else would you like to see?"

"The fields round about the village and the trees."

"Yes, they are a sight to see now, all green and flushed with grain. This will be a good year. And the trees, the mango trees, and the jack fruit trees, and the palm trees, all these are full of fruit now. I suppose you have seen them all before that way. During the last four years the fields were all dry and the trees were letting their leaves fall, but now they are again as you have seen them years ago when you had your sight. And I think you would like to see also the irrigation lake. It is full now."

"Yes, I have seen it full years ago."

"Well, it is that way now. And what else would you like to see?"

"Well, this is about all that I would like to see."

"But you have told me that you have seen it all before and you know how everything looks, and I can assure you that it does not look much different from what it has looked years ago, even fifty years ago, when I came around here with that padrae who had a beard."

"So you know the tadikaran (the man with the beard)?"

"Yes, he was a friend and brother of mine. Well, then, what for do you want to see this all again if you have seen it all before and know how it is?"

"You are right, friend."

"But have you ever heard that there are things to be seen even without eyes in the head? And that these things which can be seen without eyes in the head are much more important, and some of them much more beautiful, than those which we see with the eyes in the head?"

"How is that possible, and what are some things that a man may see without eyes in the head?"

"They are the things which God has prepared for them who love Him, and God opens up eyes in their inside so that they may see those things which God wants them to see. Things which eye has not seen and ear has not heard and which have not entered man's heart. God makes men see and hear and experience in their hearts."

"How does God open up eyes in the inside?"

"That is a good question, friend, you have asked there, a question which should interest not only you but all those who stand around. Hence, please, you all listen to the answer to this question: How does God open up eyes in the inside of us so that we all may see things we have as yet not seen?

"I have just said God does that. Of course God, who does that, is not Hanuman, who stands in stone in your temple. That one is the image of a monkey, and you all know what a monkey can do and not do. God, who can open eyes in the inside of a man, is the almighty creator of heaven and earth, the One who lets the sun shine and sends rain to make the fruits of the field grow. He is our Father, the One who gave us body and life and soul and who keeps us well and to whom we will again have to return. Him we cannot see with the eyes in our head; hence, you who cannot see with the eyes of the head are not worse off than all of us. None has ever seen God, but we know He is there. He has not left Himself without witness. Even our own inside tells us that there is a God who governs and guides all things. He is the One who must open the inside eyes in us that we may know Him right. Now, how does He open the inner eye? You have heard of hospitals and how the doctors some times open up the inside of a man to see what sickness he has and to help him. They use a knife to cut into the inside. God does not do so when He wants to enter our inside to open the inner eye. He does not use a knife made of steel, but He uses something which is even sharper than steel and cuts, although it is not like anything with which we cut. He opens the inner eye with His Word."

"God has spoken?" the blind man asked incredulously.

"Yes, God has spoken; He has spoken to men, and men have written down His Word, and here it is printed. Feel this little book, it is a part of the Word of God. You, of course, cannot read because you cannot see with the eyes in the head and in this you are not worse [off] than many who have eyes in their heads but have never used their eyes to see and learn the Word of God, which is a great pity. But you and all who cannot read can hear His Word. His Word is now in my mouth and I bring it to you. And with it He opens your heart and makes in it new eyes that you can see that which you have never seen and will never see unless you listen."

Again the blind man interjected: "Through God's Word what will you first see?"

"You will first see yourself, not how long or short your nose is, or whether your hair is black or white, or whether your loin cloth is clean or dirty. No, you will see and find out what is going on in your inside, in your heart. You will see how you really are in the sight of God and learn what God thinks of you. We all know what other people think of us. Some think good of us, others think bad of us. And we all know how we ourselves think of us. We all think of ourselves as good, at least that we are as good as the other people are. But it is of the greatest importance that we see ourselves just as God sees us, for He is the One before whom we will have to stand one day. Upon His judgment of us will depend whether we go to Yamalacham or to Sorgam [to hell or heaven]. And He is the One who knows all, also the hidden things and thoughts of the heart and mind. Nothing can we cover so that He might not see it. All the present, the past, and the future, all is ever present before Him. Hence He has a true picture of us. He knows how we are in reality. He knows us better than we know ourselves and better than other people know us.

"Now, what does He say in His word about you and me and all of us here? He says — and please pay attention all of you who stand near here, and there a little too far off. Come a little nearer — 'There is none righteous, no, not one. There is none that understandeth, there is none that seeketh after God. They are all gone out of the way. They are together become unprofitable. There is none that doeth good, no, not one. With their tongues they have used deceit. Their mouth is full of cursing and bitterness. The way of peace they have not known. There is no fear of God before their eyes. All have sinned and come short of the glory of God.' So that is what God sees in us: nothing good. We all have sinned as criminals before God. And what happens to a criminal before the magistrate's court? He is punished. . . . Since we stand as criminals before God, we too deserve punishment. And what is God's punishment for such as we are, who cared nothing for God, did not fear Him, did not even try to know him? 'The man that sinned he shall die.' That is God's punishment. Death! Not only this death which we all know when life leaves the body, but eternal death in hell. Dying forever, experiencing the pains of death, and never coming to an end. Eternal damnation. 'Ayyoooh!' My hair stands straight on my head when I think of it. But when God through His Word opens our inner eye, we begin to see more than this sad picture of ourselves. God permits us to look into His own heart."

The blind man, somewhat perplexed, asked, "God permits us to see into His own heart? Does He do such a thing?"

"Yes, He does so and we thank Him that He has done so. We look into the heart of God, which He opens to us in His Word. What do we see there with the eye of our heart? We see that He does not delight in the death and damnation of a sinner. He does not like to see us go to Yamalacham and there to suffer forever. He pities us as a father pities his children when he sees them going wrong. And He does more than pity us. He wishes and desires that we should live, live with Him in eternal bliss and happiness. He not only wishes that we should live, but in His good will, mercy, and grace saves us from death and damnation. . . . How does he save us? The way of salvation He has also made known to us in His Word. And I pray that He may open our eyes, the eyes of our understanding and of our heart, the inner eye, that we may see this way of salvation. It is the only one. Many ways may go to Madras, but only one goes to heaven. Here is His way of salvation for us all, blind and seeing ones, sick and healthy ones, white people and brown people. Here is His way of salvation which you must see if you wish to be eternally happy with the Father in heaven. 'God so loved the world,' you and me and everybody, 'that He gave His only son, that whosoever believes in Him should not perish but have everlasting life.' "

Henry was very intent to drive home especially this part of the message, for he was convinced that this same message which had saved him from death would save these people to whom he talked in the village square. God's Son, he continued, "became man and as man took the name of Jesus Christ, which means the anointed Savior of man. He was born without sin of a virgin woman who had known no man. God with His almighty power and in His infinite wisdom created in the womb of a pure woman, who had never slept with a man, a pure, sinless child, Jesus, His son, God's own son. He was like us in everything except sin. He was holy, harmless, undefiled, separate from sinners, made higher than the heavens.

"He, Jesus, the Savior, did for us, what we ourselves could never do. He did right in everything. He lived fully and completely, always according to His father's will. He stepped into our place. We are to live according to God's will, what we were to do and could not, He did for us, in our place and in our stead. What He did, God in His Grace counts as done by us. Thus He fulfilled everything God wanted us to fulfill but never did fulfill. And more He did. He took our wrongs, our bad deeds and words and thoughts, in short, our sins upon Himself. He bore our sins in His body like a burden bearer bears the burden which presses hard upon the head of those who carry baskets to the market and also suffered the punishment for our sins. He did not die for His sins. He had none. He died for ours. And thus He redeemed us with His holy life and His innocent suffering and death. He was buried and on the third day . . . He rose again from the dead and now lives and reigns forever. He is the way, the truth and the life. He that believes on Him, though he were dead, yet shall he live again.

"That is the way to heaven. Jesus Christ. He is your God and Savior. He that accepts Him as his God and Savior shall not perish but have everlasting life. I pray to God that He may open in you eyes to see yourselves as you really stand before God that you may look into the heart of God and there see His infinite love for you and that you may behold, in Jesus, your Savior and follow Him."

The blind man retorted, "Teacher, you know that when you want to drive a nail into a board it will not go in with one blow of the hammer. You must give it five, six, ten blows. So it is with what you have said. You must tell us this again and again. Perchance it will enter into our hearts. We are glad you came and told us what no one else tells us. Come again when the moon shines and many more people will be here."

Village talks like these were delivered again and again by Henry and his associates as they moved day by day among the people in Vaniyambadi. The approach might change due to variation in the situations they encountered, but the message was always the same. Henry was a convinced Christian and a man of great intelligence. He knew of no better news. God's own story was his mission. It was his inspiration.

CHAPTER 27

In 1952, drought sapped the land around Vaniyambadi, causing crops to shrivel and the people to go hungry. Many other regions of South India suffered from want. To help fight the famine at Vaniyambadi, Henry urged the mission board members in the States not to send food packages but to rush money. With money, the missionaries could buy the supplies they knew would best fit the needs of the people. The treasurer of the Mohammedan Mission Society forwarded immediately a check for $300. Gratefully, Henry assured his superiors that he would buy staples such as rice and other cereals to feed the people and avoid the waste that usually occurred when shipping foods from America to India.

At the end of 1952 Henry visited 42 villages, bringing with him either by spoken word or through tracts the message of Christmas. In one village a cholera epidemic had afflicted many of the Christian residents and a number of Muslims whom Henry had been evangelizing. Without discriminating, Henry distributed 250 cholera pills to the sick. To purchase these pills, he used $30 that had been donated to the mission. He was quick to assure the donors that the money was used not only to combat the cholera epidemic but also to further the advance of the gospel.

At times, his own coworkers scolded Henry for what they considered to be instances of indiscreet liberality, but they all knew why he gave so freely. He would tell them, "Better to err on the side of generosity than on the side of stinginess." Such generosity he never lavished on himself. It was his habit always to open his hand widest when he thought of others.

Every hour of daylight was so filled with work that Henry and his coworkers, including Ernest Hahn who joined the force in 1952, had to offer 24-hour service. He would joke with friends saying, "This missionary business is an around-the-clock operation. I am the daytime manager, at your service from five in the morning until five in the afternoon. Hahn is the night manager. He takes the helm from five in the afternoon until five in the morning. For all who are interested, we're open 24 hours." The sober dedication which such jokes modestly concealed became the bedrock of the reputation Henry and his coworkers won throughout the church. During the general conference of the Lutheran Church in 1954 a layman from Bombay, who became a Christian while living in America, urged the Lutherans to begin working in Bombay and the teeming regions close by. Enthusiastic for the beginning of such a project, he pointed out that Bombay "needed a man like Henry Nau who has no reverse gear."

Henry was anxious to sustain his Indian colleagues' loyalty to mission duties. Twice a week, he took with him a group of these brothers to visit the villages scattered around Vaniyambadi. The work started at six o'clock in the morning and often continued late into the morning until it became too hot. Henry inspired loyalty to mission work. Even Samraj, the headmaster of the mission's higher elementary school, was enchanted by Henry's magic. Samraj became so thrilled to work among the Muslims that he left the elementary school and became a missionary and zealous evangelist. Many of the young missionaries, who carried on the work in India after Henry's return to America, believed that the most enduring contribution of his final short stay in India was the excitement he aroused among native Christians to bring the gospel to the Muslims and Hindus.

Before he left India, he was privileged to rest briefly at Kodaikanal in the coolness of the hill country. He needed this break from his endless round of obligation although always eager to return to the action, explaining, "I'm glad to be back in the plains where the excitement is and I can recuperate from my stay in the hills. The hotter the weather, the better I work."

Like the Indian colleagues, Ernest Hahn enjoyed Henry's spacious hospitality. Ernest lived in the house at the lower end of the Lutheran compound. He often walked up the hill to talk with Henry and Helen. Through such talks, Ernest realized that Henry was thoroughly consumed by enthusiasm for the work of the kingdom. He was also pleased that Henry, although older, more seasoned, and exceptionally talented in languages, treated him and his wife as equals. Henry always welcomed the suggestions of the inexperienced younger man.

Shortly after Henry and Helen had arrived in India, they celebrated their forty-fifth wedding anniversary on November 12, 1951. They were in Krishnagiri, the town where they were married in 1906. From their lodging in the town Henry and Helen strolled to a familiar chapel. Entering, they walked up the aisle and knelt at the altar rail. Memories of their wedding day when they had first knelt together at this altar rail began to overwhelm them. That occasion was marked by a grand feast and by a house full of well-wishing guests. Now, alone in God's presence, they thanked Him for His blessings throughout their many years as husband and wife. They retraced their lives together while working in India, suffering and serving in Germany, planning in the United States, venturing into Africa, and now returning in their old age to serve in the land of their first love. Helen and Henry shed tears of joy and gratitude.

Years earlier Henry had written an article entitled: "The Footprints of God." Little did he and Helen realize at the time that the words would prove to be a description of their own event-filled lives. God's direction of Jonathan Udoe Ekong to Greensboro was as miraculous as the guidance He provided for Henry, both before and after his marriage to Helen. Now here they were to renew their marriage vows.

Helen whispered, "Henry, I love you and pledge loyalty and love to you until death do us part." Henry responded, "Helen, I pledge my love . . ." He paused. Images in a stream meandered from a source hidden in his memory. Here was his father looking so haggard. The anxiety of endlessly disciplining Henry, his unruly boy, had worn the old man down. His father's image faded, and other images congealed. Here was a young man, strutting audaciously in bright, gaudy costume. Henry recognized the profligate gambler he had been between 1901 and 1903. Neither Helen nor any of their children had yet known about these years; it was Henry's secret, and Helen would never need to know. Because of his faith in God's mercy, the memory of them no longer harassed Henry's conscience. God had forgiven him because Jesus was sacrificed.

In this silent chapel, a man and a woman spoke their love to one another as they looked back on 45 years together in the service of their Redeemer from sin, who had made them children of God. God had mercifully chosen a man like Henry to be His servant and messenger to many people throughout the world. Here was a man of mission — loyal and inspiring loyalty in others.

CHAPTER 28

As 1954 approached, Henry prepared to return to the United States. Unexpectedly, word came from the president of the St. Louis Seminary, Alfred O. Fuerbringer, that the faculty had voted to bestow upon him an honorary Doctorate of Divinity. The honor was in recognition of his outstanding service as a missionary of the Lutheran church while in India, in America, and in Nigeria, as well as of his leadership in publicizing the church's mission program, particularly through the Society for the Promotion of Mohammedan Missions.

The faculty wanted the church and the world to know that God had done much through Henry Nau and that many people had come to appreciate God's gifts to the church by witnessing the dedication of this man, inspired with mission. When he received the news, Henry hesitated to accept the honor because many others seemed to him more deserving.

Memories of stormy encounters while serving as president of Immanuel arose to reproach him: heated discussions with colleagues and superiors, and even the threats of several resignations. He recalled some of the occasions when he felt compelled to apologize after vehement disagreements over what he considered to be priorities of the kingdom. In the late forties he had wanted to be the first chairman of the mission department at the seminary but had failed to receive the position. Many important people in the synod had reservations about him. Yet here was the faculty of the Synod's most prestigious school ready to present this stormy petrel with its highest award. Instead of making friends, he had earned enemies because of his impartiality and compelling enthusiasm. However, when Helen pleaded with him to consider the good intentions and feelings of the many people he would otherwise hurt, Henry accepted. At the graduation exercises of the class of 1954 he received the Doctor of Divinity degree. *In absentia,* the program read. On that day he was in the Middle East, 73 years old and, for the second time in his life, somebody.

Just before leaving India, Henry was instructed by the Foreign Mission Board to stop over in Beirut, Lebanon. He accepted the assignment to visit Beirut as a likely spot to begin Christian mission work through radio broadcasting. Henry left for Lebanon only after the assurance that additional workers, missionaries, and medical aides would be on their way to continue the work he had started among the Muslims of Southern India. After three years' absence, Helen was unhappy that the separation from her children and grandchildren would be prolonged by a stay in Lebanon. She wanted to hasten home. Therefore, when Henry and Helen arrived in Port Said in mid-April, 1954, they bade each other good-bye. He went on to Beirut, arriving there in May. Helen continued on to New York.

In the course of a hectic tour that lasted until June 14, Henry again assessed the practicality of missionary work in Lebanon, particularly in Beirut. He was not keen about beginning work in Lebanon. Already while immersed in the work at Vaniyambadi he expressed the view that Christian missionaries were needed more urgently in Muslim lands other than Lebanon. Lebanon was considered an Arab country, and yet Roman Catholics, Syrian Christians, and other Christian groups made up 51 percent of the population. In his opinion there were more Christian missions in Lebanon than in any other Muslim country, whereas the work among the Muslims in India had just begun and was still staffed inadequately. "It was important," he said, "not to dissipate the Lutheran effort and thus weaken the work in India while still in its infancy." The fact that his motto at this time, "Dig in, don't spread out," seemed to be in conflict with his own vision of a cosmic evangelism program within his own lifetime apparently did not occur to Henry.

Prior to this tour of Lebanon, Henry had written to the mission board stressing that work among the Muslims could not be done in "Pentecostal" fashion but required years of solid preparation. Islam was a strong competitor, with a coherent dogmatic rationale and equitable civil laws. Its enterprising ministry was well prepared with prayer services for every Friday and with fraternal orders which were more effective than any Christian counterpart of which Henry had knowledge. A decision should not be hastily made to charge into Lebanon to work among the Muslims. He explained that whirlwind visits by synodical officials to any proposed mission field only gave superficial impressions and were an inadequate basis for responsible decisions. Apart from these objections, he knew that the political unrest he had seen during his last visit had not yet been quieted. Henry reminded the board: "I know what I'm talking about. I've been there."

Henry left Beirut on June 21, 1954. A month later, on the nineteenth of July, he was in St. Louis reporting to the Foreign Mission Board of the Lutheran Church-Missouri Synod on the work among the Muslims in India. During the meeting the board asked for his assessment of the practicality of starting work in Beirut. Henry frankly discouraged such an effort. The area, he explained, offered only limited opportunities for evangelism.

After the meeting Henry returned to his home in Greensboro. There on West Green Court, he relaxed with Helen. Friends from the Mission Society and other interested people visited him daily, usually to discuss the purpose and methods of foreign mission work. The backyard became Henry's favorite sanctuary. There he liked to sit and sample ripe persimmons from a laden tree nearby. The unsightly tree owed its upright condition solely to the fact that it satisfied Henry's craving for its succulent fruit. The lush fragrance of Helen's well-manicured flower beds soothed Henry while touring his hidden retreat.

To break the monotony of too much leisure, Henry wrote a series of mission talks. They were intended to instruct seminarians and young missionaries how to tell the followers of Allah the good news about Jesus. Also, late in the year, he completed ten village talks similar to the simple talk he gave in Krishnagiri.

Henry tried to keep busy, but he was not happy staying in Greensboro. In his opinion he was only dawdling at home. By the spring of 1955 restlessness had gnawed on him enough. He asked Helen if she would like to go with him on a new assignment to Cuba or Jamaica, or maybe — if he was needed — to Guatemala. Meekly, Helen answered that she would be happy to go to Cuba or Jamaica. But Guatemala? "Not for me," she said. She would, however, assent to an assignment in Mexico if anyone was needed there. Henry wrote his board, advising them that if he should be needed in any of these countries, he was more than ready to go. To the board's surprise, he also heartily volunteered for another tour of duty in India.

While on a speaking tour in St. Louis, Nau was introduced to the audience as a missionary emeritus. He countered, "I do not at all feel like an emeritus missionary, because I desire to get into the work again!" The drive in this man was tremendous. Inspired in mission, he was a constant inspiration to others.

Before he had left India, Henry had written to friends in America asking them to arrange speaking tours in much of the United States. His brother, J. Henry, programmed an extensive lecture circuit throughout Wisconsin. Henry traversed the state, electrifying congregations with his proclamation of the vital need for evangelism of the Muslims in India. In June he toured central Illinois, stopping at Jacksonville, Loda, Lincoln, Siegel, Vandalia, Effingham, Altamont, Petersburg, and Broadlands. In August he was in South Dakota; in September, Iowa; in October, Ohio; and in November, North Dakota.

Although he sometimes grumbled about what seemed to him a slow pace, 1955 was one of Henry's most active years. It also marked an important milestone, of which he took scant notice. Fifty years had passed since he had been ordained into the ministry of the Lutheran Church-Missouri Synod. In response to his fifty years of service as missionary, teacher, and pastor, congratulations poured in from around the world. These unexpected kind words, especially the congratulations from the members of his Foreign Mission Board, moved Henry. He wrote to the board,

Nothing outstanding nor extraordinary nor praiseworthy has been done. If I looked at what the Lord has done during the fifty years of my life, I am greatly humbled and must confess that often I have not measured up to what He required of me and what those who had called me into the Lord's service expected of me. Hence, far from exulting today, I am deeply sorry that the long time the Lord has granted me in His service has not been better utilized.

These words were from the heart of a man called by God to a mission. Always looking for the opportunity to spread the Gospel, Henry had no time to wait for praise. When a gift of $100 arrived from the members of the board, he was pleasantly surprised, but graciously accepted the money. Quietly he thanked God for the Lord's safekeeping of his family and himself throughout the many years. Trusting in God, Henry had come to terms with time. Today was all that mattered. Tomorrow was always too late. And yesterday was not a time to ponder.

By this time, when Henry was old and his work almost finished, one important problem had been resolved. Finally he felt at ease with members of a board. Now, in association with the members of the Foreign Mission Board of the Missouri Synod, he felt more like a partner than a staff orderly. He expressed his thankfulness to his colleagues in these words:

It has been a continuous pleasure to have worked with you and under your guidance. You have had always an open ear for any requests on my part and a ready heart and an open hand to assist and help wherever and whenever it was needed. God bless you one and all.

Such affable words were never written to the members of the Mission Board of the Synodical Conference under whose authority he had chafed throughout much of his career at Immanuel College. About them he once bitterly said: "The Holy Spirit lived only in St. Louis and then seemed to be dressed in a policeman's uniform."

Some of Henry's clashes with the Synodical Conference Board might well have been due to conflicting personalities, divergent perspective in policy-making, and deficient trust in relationships. But Henry refused to dwell on the reasons, and his rather generous appraisal of his later relationship with the Missouri Synod board suggests that the vinegar in his soul had undergone a mellowing process.

Although Henry was now in the twilight of his years, he wanted most of all to work. Again he heard rumors that he might be asked to be a professor in the School of Missions at Concordia Seminary, but no official word came and his hopes were dashed. In September, 1955 he learned that he might be needed in Guatemala, but nothing came of that either. To gain an assignment, he talked with Herman H. Koppelmann, chairman of the Missouri Synod's Board of Foreign Missions: "I am prepared to return to India for another two years. Whether in Muslim mission, whether in Tamil or Malayalam — it makes no difference to me. I just want to go back, preferably in January of 1956. I plan to go alone while Helen remains in the States, for reasons we both have approved." Henry explained that his age, now 75, would probably place a limitation of two years on his stay in India. He even discussed salary: $193.00 a month was sufficient, provided that he had the same living arrangement as in 1951. Since Helen would not be going, he was not sure whether the board would pay the same $255.00 per month he made presently. But if it was agreeable to the board, he told Koppelmann, he would send Helen $155.00 a month and use the remaining $100.00 (approximately 470 rupees) for himself.

While at home waiting for news of an assignment, Henry completed a history of the joint Lutheran mission to India from 1905 to 1915, which was the second decade of mission work by the Missouri Synod. Though writing about past events, Henry kept in mind the relevance of this history for the present. It was of utmost importance, he insisted, that a missionary should not divert his energies to secondary tasks, such as managing bookstores, presses, hospitals, or operating picture shows. In Henry's judgment, all these tasks had little to do with real mission contact. Too much machinery and organization diverted the attention of the missionary and the church away from direct outreach to the Indian masses. Evangelism should be the missionaries' specialty. Whether aimed at individuals or groups, evangelism should be a cooperative work between the missionary and the Indian clergy, teachers, and laity, it was to have priority rating.

A missionary should not be expected to be responsible for the total management of mission schools. It would be far better to have him teach. Thereby he would develop further insight into the place of the school in the total mission enterprise; and he could cement bonds between himself and the pupils that could endure many years.

Whatever alienated the missionary from his Indian coworkers was to be eliminated as quickly as possible, Henry admonished. The missionary and his family should feel they belong to and are an integral part of the local congregation and should not consider themselves superior in any way. Evangelism was to take priority in the mission budget. No one, particularly the missionary and his family, ought to ask for more money than was needed. Because Henry had lived in India, he knew that envy is best avoided by equality. The missionary's standard of living should approximate the simple means of his Indian colleagues.

These were only a few of his more practical suggestions and were associated with his views on the policy-making power of Stateside boards and committees. On the basis of long experience he was convinced that responsibility for decisions in these and other matters would be most effectively made by missionaries in the field and in cooperation with the local Christians.

Once Henry got an idea it usually remained a fixture. A case in point was his adamant position as to the best choice of locale for the spending of mission dollars. On one occasion, the Board of Directors of the Missouri Synod had slotted some of the money from the Synod's centennial contributions for mission work in Japan and South America. Henry responded to the board's decision by firing a broadside. In *The Minaret,* he wrote:

> Why set aside money for two unsanctioned mission projects and why exclude any other which is at least of equal importance if not of greater importance?

Then he answered his own question with extended advice:

> We do not begrudge a single dollar which will go into Japanese or South American missions. Japan needs Christian missions, but Japan has been a mission field for almost a hundred years and practically every American denomination is on the field. The Lutheran church is on the field. Even an indigenous Japanese church is on the field. Also in South America we see a great need for Christian missions, for the darkness in Roman Catholic countries is as dense as in heathen lands. Let us charge the Lutheran church in Brazil and Argentina with the task of bringing the gospel into Chile, Peru, Equador, and other South American republics. Let us subsidize the church there if it has not the means; but it is their work, their duty and their responsibility. Why must we crowd into an occupied field when there are virgin fields galore? When once we, as a church, can catch the vision of a new day in missions, then the barren lands of Islam, the grazing grounds of the Somali Nomads, the wide plains of Sinkiang, the rugged mountains of the Kurds, and the banks of the Mekong no longer will frighten but beckon and entice us. Let us deliberately and boldly choose the difficult and dangerous, the unevangelized, the neediest fields for our synod's second hundred years of foreign mission endeavor.

Another incident illustrates that Henry did not easily compromise his opinions. A professor at Duke University in Durham, North Carolina, laced into Henry for using *The Minaret* to present only the dark side of mission work among the Muslims. This scholar felt that Henry should have balanced the picture with a description of the more alluring aspects of mission work. Included in this description should have been such wonders as the desert with its burning sands towering like the waves of a storm. Also worthy of verbal celebration, he felt, was the official reception accorded visiting dignitaries by King Ibin Saud of Saudi Arabia: the cauldrons of boiling rice and mutton, the black tents of Kedar, the buntings in all the colors of the rainbow that flutter atop the tents, the camels drowsing beside the tents, and the famous Rolls Royce of the King. Henry replied:

> When we have gotten the missionary into the Muslim mission fields by such flattery and he finds that this bright side is nothing but a will o'-the-wisp, a fanciful figment of the imagination, what then? Will he not justly condemn us as men who willfully misrepresented the field and got him into it by lies and deceits? No, dear brother, I think it is better to tell the truth, that our missionary be forewarned. Then every little rose he finds will be a joyous discovery. Every pleasant experience will be received with thanksgiving. He will, through his joyous experience, receive a new stimulus to greater exertion in the work of the Lord.

Although Henry had challenged his colleague's views, he realized that in a certain sense the man was correct. In a subsequent communication he called attention to what he had always considered the really positive aspect of mission commitment: "The bright side was not being alone. The Lord was with the missionary, and He also would find others that were willing to give their lives and to spend their time and effort to learn (about) different peoples, cultures, and to live an adventurous life."

Henry was not only loyal to the sober work of spreading the gospel, he was also a staunch Lutheran. Zahora, an Indian friend, once asked him, "Are you a Protestant minister?" Henry boomed, "Absolutely! You see, I am a Lutheran. We Lutherans are always leading the way when it comes to being a Protestant."

Puzzled, Zahora queried, "What is a Lutheran? Is Lutheran Protestant?"

Henry expounded, "Now see here, Zahora, I'll explain this thing to you. As Protestants the Lutherans are the genuine article, the real thing. Well, what I mean is that they were the first Protestants there ever were. A long, long time ago there was a diet in Spires. Spires is a town in Germany and a diet is a congress, a convention, a large meeting. And at this one they talked about religion. There were two sides, and the main man on the one side was Luther. That was where they started calling some people Protestants, those people that followed Luther. They call these people Lutherans now. So you see, a Lutheran is right up in the front line when it comes to being a Protestant."

Zahora sounded convinced: "Oh, I am so glad that you are a Protestant!"

CHAPTER 29

Busy as he was in 1955, Henry broke with custom and took the time to visit most of his children. He had to skip Henry Richard, because a trip to distant California was too expensive.

Walter was chairman of the Department of Romance Languages at Lenoir Rhyne College, in Hickory, North Carolina, and appreciated his father's occasional assistance. When Henry visited Walter and his family, he would teach the Spanish, French, and Portuguese classes for a few weeks. Henry enjoyed this change of routine.

Since Mary Ann and Irene lived close to Greensboro, Henry was able to see them a bit more often. Eric lived right in Greensboro and naturally saw his parents more frequently than did any of the other children.

Henry was invited in May to speak at the graduation exercises of the Lutheran Academy and College in Selma, Alabama. This offer he accepted gladly. He immediately wrote John, who had taken residence in Hattiesburg, Mississippi, about the speaking engagement. If John would drive to Selma, Henry hoped he might return with John to Hattiesburg and see his grandchildren whom he had not seen for many years. John met him in Selma and from there they drove to Hattiesburg.

The days passed swiftly, until it was time for Henry to return home. Only after long embraces and sorrowful good-byes did they let Henry go. Johanna, John's wife, observed after Henry left, "Opa doesn't look like himself. He must be working too hard."

At the turn of the year Henry Nau had seen 75 winters. The year 1956 was the year he hoped to return to India, if necessary without Helen, so completely had his commitment to mission work saturated every vein in his body.

The days of January were snatched one by one from the calendar. Henry waited for his mission board to give the signal for his departure to India. He waited day in and day out through February.

One afternoon an urgent request came from Walter, who asked Henry to teach his language classes at Lenoir Rhyne while he attended a convention of language professors in California. This appeal arrived at a time when Henry needed a reprieve from fretting over his pending overseas trip. He accepted and went with Helen to Hickory where they lived in Walter's house. Henry was delighted by the students in Walter's classes, and they in turn appreciated Henry, particularly his skill as a philologist. Every morning he strolled to the campus, drilled his classes, and returned home by noon. Afternoons and evenings were free. "So this is an academician's life at a white college," commented Henry as he enjoyed an agreeable respite.

One lunch break, about a week after he came to Hickory, Henry walked stiffly into the house and muttered, "Helen, my chest . . . it hurts." Helen urged, "Rest here on the lounge in the living room." A brief rest, she hoped, would help the pain to subside. She offered him lunch, but he refused to eat. "Better give me a cup of coffee," he said. The afternoon wore on; at two o'clock there was no improvement; and at four his condition was worse. Helen finally realized that the pains were centered around the heart and at about six o'clock she rushed to a neighbor for help. The neighbor ran back to the house with Helen. He examined Henry and immediately called the hospital for an ambulance. A doctor arrived with the ambulance and quickly diagnosed the pain as a severe heart attack. The ambulance attendants packed Henry onto a stretcher and hurriedly drove him to the hospital where he was placed in an oxygen tent.

All his children came to see him. Henry Richard flew from California to be at his father's bedside. The children and Helen were cheered by the news that the resiliency of his well-exercised body gave Henry a better than 50 percent chance to live. One doctor, who was a friend of the family and had been at Conover Preparatory School with John, stated the problem this way: "If we can get his water works to function, he'll be all right." The water works were fixed and Henry began to recover. The boys, who had journeyed far to be with their father, bade him farewell. With a flickering smile and an unfinished wave of his left hand, he assured them that he would pull through.

By late March Henry rode home to Greensboro in an ambulance. Six weeks had passed in the hospital at Hickory. Now, in his old surroundings, he made excellent progress. When the weather became more gentle in April, he was allowed to leave his bed and take in the refreshing air and sunshine in the backyard. The tidy gardens were evidence of Helen's love for flowers and shrubbery. Doctor Carl Durham called on his missionary friend every day. Many more friends, both black and white, were permitted to visit Henry by early May. From around the world, wishes for a speedy recovery arrived. Thousands of Christians were praying for him.

Despite his illness, Henry would not resign himself to passivity. What worried him most was that he might never see India again. When people visited Henry, he talked with much spirit about his plans for new mission projects. He could not relinquish his hope for an active role in these plans, and so the doctor's prescription of pleasant small talk went unheeded. A life of leisure was not his style.

Long discussion with friends about the future mission of the Church continued to fill the days of Henry's recovery. He carried on with as much energy as his health permitted. Friends knew that a last tour of duty was Henry's greatest wish. "I want to get back to India, just once more."

Strength seemed to return to Henry. Then a second heart attack struck without warning in early May. This time he refused to go to the hospital. Helen and Mary Ann, after consultation with Dr. Durham, decided to honor Henry's request. He remained in his bed at home.

Henry had often marvelled over the way his heavenly Father had taken control of his life and given him the privilege of sharing in the Great Commission. Now a new set of orders, not voted by the board in St. Louis, Missouri, was on the way. Henry Nau was about to embark on the tour for which he had often told others that provision had been made "before the foundation of the world." At four o'clock in the afternoon, on Thursday, May 17, 1956, Henry's last words to Helen were, "I'm going home."

The funeral service was simple. Friends gathered at Ebenezer Lutheran Church on May 20 at three o'clock in the afternoon. They came from all walks of life, rich and poor, white and black, literate and illiterate. In the place of tears, a song of triumph, in celebration of Henry's homecoming, swelled from the congregation. The man of mission was dead, but the worshipers knew his spirit would march on and inspire many with commitment to God's mission.

Leslie Frerking, of Charlotte, committed Nau's body to the grave. Valiantly he had worked with Henry in arousing the church to bring the Good News to the Muslims. Quietly he read the words that give ultimate meaning to the Great Commission: "Earth to earth, ashes to ashes, dust to dust, in the hope of the resurrection of the flesh through our Lord Jesus Christ."

Now Henry lay beside his beloved daughter, Esther, in the Forest Lawn Cemetery at the Guilford County Courthouse Battlefield, in North Carolina. A simple headstone marked his grave: "Where I am, there shall also my servant be."

EPILOGUE

Eight days after Henry's burial, Mary Ann received a letter of condolence from Herman H. Koppelmann, with whom Henry had often corresponded. His words expressed the thoughts that were in the minds and hearts not only of those who had attended the funeral but of others, throughout the world, who had heard of Nau's death:

> Last Saturday as I was listening to a program from radio station KFUO, St. Louis, I heard the verse that has become very familiar with our city missions, which ends along this thought, that when a person gets to heaven, he hopes he will meet someone there who will say, "It was you who invited me here." I am sure your father is also having that joyous experience with many souls from many parts of this globe of ours. I know that even in the midst of your sorrow you rejoice in the great work the Lord permitted him and the successes He permitted him to have.

To know the man one had to see him in action, both in word and in deed. On the one hand, Nau was a professional man, dedicated to his work. At the same time he was responsible for a family and the maintenance of a house. It was not easy for him to keep the two roles in balance.

Helen and the children knew him as provider and disciplinarian. Born September 13, 1885, Helen was only 20 when she went to India to become the wife of missionary Nau. Henry's relations with her were often dictated by a German's idea of womanhood: *Kinder, Kueche, und Kirche.* That is, a woman ought to bear children, cook, and attend church faithfully. At times Henry could be very inconsiderate of Helen's feelings. On occasion, when her own better opinion was not honored, she would retire to the bedroom and have a good cry.

Because of her husband's frequent absences, she had more than her share of the upbringing of their children. She was especially close to her three daughters. When they were in their teens, she attended baseball games, marathon dance contests, and other amusements with them and was regularly informed about the progress of their love life.

She enjoyed a good relationship also with her sons and impressed on them the importance of self-discipline. In 1926 her son John attended school in Conover. He returned quite homesick at Christmas time, with no intention of going back. Helen told him, "You have said A; now you must say B." John continued his studies.

Henry was very strict with his children, and Helen thought that often his punishments were excessive. In her own way she would remove some of the sting. When, for example, one of the children was sent to bed without supper, Helen would slip food to the child.

Although Helen's gentle persuasion did manage to trim the sharper edges of Henry's household reign, Teutonic tradition retained a firm grip on Nau. He maintained that the first-born son should be the privileged one. This was known as the principle of primogeniture. Walter was to bear the family tradition. Henry and Helen confided in him more than in any of the other children, including Eric, to whom Henry felt especially close.

When Walter earned his doctorate from Duke University, Nau arranged a banquet to honor his son. To commemorate the occasion, he passed on to Walter the doctor's gown which colleagues in the Southeastern District had given him years earlier. Proudly and magnanimously Henry promised: "Should any other son of mine [he forgot the girls entirely] attain a doctorate, he also will receive a gown from me." In 1954 John, his third-born, qualified for his father's prize. But by then Nau, who was reputed to have had the memory of an elephant, somehow forgot his promise and followed the tradition of primogeniture.

Nau always worried about his family's financial condition. There simply was not enough money to go around. Seldom did her children ask to see a movie in town, but when they did, Helen suggested that they go to their father for the money. The brood voted on their spokesperson. As head of the delegation, this unlucky party was charged with the task of requesting the admission money from Father. Henry would be in his study absorbed in reading. The delegation would enter and the elected sibling would cough politely. When she got to the word "money," Father would jump from his seat as if an electric current had passed through him. "Money for a show? I haven't got a dime."

Once, when John was seventeen and away at college, he wrote home for $3 to buy a second-hand suit. Henry answered:

> Dear John: Your request for three dollars has come to my attention. I would love to give you $3. In fact, I would love to give you $100, but I have neither.
>
> You must therefore do without the suit. Love, Papa

It was written, as usual, on a penny postal card.

Why this anxiety about money? Nau simply lacked good money sense. How to earn an extra dollar was a topic not covered in his books. He never read a word in the *Wall Street Journal* or any other financial periodical. Why should he? He had no money to invest. Besides, he was too busy to worry about what happened on the New York Stock Exchange. Henry thought "moonlighting" was another word for adolescent romance. Once indeed he did alert his mission board that he would have to find an extra job to supplement the inadequate salary he was receiving at Immanuel. This was, at best, a bluff. He could have done some farming on the side and done it well. But then his mission in life would have suffered. So he surrendered to the prevailing system of ecclesiastical indenture. He did teach some German to two students who were doing graduate work at Tulane University, but he regarded this as somewhat unprofessional.

The one time that Nau entered the business world was a disaster. He talked his son Eric into forming a partnership with a German baker. The business failed and Eric was out $400. Herr Rothenberg knew how to bake, but knew nothing about business. Nau knew how to work for God but not how to make money work for profit. Yet he was most meticulous in handling monies provided by the church or by individuals supporting the cause of Christian mission. He could account for every penny he spent as he traveled, explored, and worked in the interest of missions.

An African missionary, Vernon Koerper, once suggested that Henry might have made some mistakes in his accounting of monies spent during the African venture. The chief financial officer of the Synodical Conference assured the brother that Henry's financial records were in order. As can be seen from a report rendered on April 10, 1951, Nau was in the habit of keeping an exact record of everything spent, even to the smallest item. His entries included 75 cents for a passport picture, $5 for passport renewal, $10 for Mrs. Nau's passport, 25 cents for recording fee, and 35 cents for registered mail, a total of $16.35.

Of greater interest and surprise were the expenditures for his Middle East trip. He had been allotted $750.00 but used only $156.00, returning a sum of almost $600.00 to the mission treasury. Members of the auditing committee of Nau's church were not accustomed to seeing budgeted money returned in such proportions and labeled Nau the "cheapest of all missionaries." Wherever he went he looked for bargains. No matter where they were sent, missionaries would require transportation at their place of work. A memo from Nau to the Mission Board would run something like this: "We might have luck and get something from the army stockpiles in Iran."

Such thriftiness extended to his personal life. He seldom paid enough attention to his dress to worry about buying clothes. If Helen had not bought him clothes, he might have lived with as little apparel and personal belongings as some of the people he served. Helen pressed his trousers, and if she had not called attention to the spots he would never have taken a suit to the cleaner. In 1933 he was wearing the same pair of glasses that he had purchased in Germany in 1905. A Lutheran optometrist in Buffalo, New York, made him a gift of a new pair.

Nau did not own an overcoat. He swore that his existence depended on 39 necessities, no more and no less. History will never know what they were; he never took time to identify them. Nau held the Guiness record for packing for a long trip. Besides his passport, ticket money, and allowance for room and board, he needed only "a comb and a toothbrush." It was even doubtful whether he used such implements regularly.

Nau had a cosmopolitan appetite and a cast-iron stomach. Exotic foods did not excite him; simple food and drink, well prepared, tickled his palate. India, Africa, Europe, Asia, and America beckoned him to partake of their cuisine. Curry, palm oil chops, yams, potatoes, pork, sauerkraut, rice, fish, goat's meat, and elephant steaks were only a few of the foods that he enjoyed. After having developed a taste for them, Nau left few turnip greens, black-eyed peas, collards, mustards, and cornbread on his plate. Henry's stomach took literally the Lord's words: "Eat and drink such things as they give." Once, in Swansboro, North Carolina, he ate some fish in a humble cottage. The fish happened to be tainted, but Nau took it in stride and slept that night, he said, "like a kitten."

To her husband's disappointment, Helen was not a good cook. She knew it, and Henry endured it. Occasionally, however, the Naus received dinner invitations, and Henry could never forget Marie Hasenkampf, a German woman in New Orleans. Schooled in the art of German-Creole cooking, she prepared food for Nau that transported him into a state of ecstasy: crab and shrimp gumbo, crawfish bisque, crab soup, oyster stew, and étoufée.

Although Nau drank water, milk, and coffee lustily, he really savored wines, especially if he had a hand in making them. On one occasion he invited his daughter-in-law, Johanna, to join him in drinking a glass of his homemade blackberry wine. She was incredulous. "Opa, why do you drink wine at ten o'clock in the morning?" He answered, "Whatever the appetite calls for, that I will eat and drink."

Strength and weaknesses mingled in Nau. Ernest Hahn declared that he knew no better story teller about mission work than Henry. On a visit to Buffalo, New York, he was guest of the Fritz Bogumil family. After addressing a large gathering at Salem Lutheran church, he returned to his host's home and entertained members of the family with his stories. Everyone there had to be at work at 7 A.M., but the hours glided by as they listened to their enchanting guest. Only the clock striking three broke Henry's spell.

Nau's weak side became especially apparent whenever he addressed audiences that were to make decisions on specific mission undertakings. He was often gruff, hard-hitting, and intolerant of ideas that did not endorse his own. "To hell with statistics in the kingdom of God! What's needed is to go and tell." From time to time he openly criticized ministers serving Ebenezer Lutheran church in Greensboro, his home congregation. He felt that they did not apply themselves with vigor to the mission of the church. When individual communion cups were used to celebrate the Lord's Supper at the conclusion of a certain conference, he shouted, "I will have none of it. The single cup symbolizes unity in Christ; and if my black brethren cannot receive communion from the common cup, neither can I."

Nau could be impetuous. Once he hurled a Bible at a catechist who angered him by asking for a life stipend. Ready for Africa, he ordered a doctor in St. Louis to lose no time in immunizing him. "I want all seven shots at once!"

In one of his conciliatory moments he grabbed Frank Lankenau and William Kampschmidt in a bear hug as the two tried to engage in fisticuffs over a misunderstanding. He urged them to settle their differences in a more Christian manner. Colleague Wisler, however, received a different lecture: "If you have nothing better to say, get off the campus and don't return. If you do, you will have me to face, and I will physically evict you from the campus."

Nau's knowledge of music was inversely commensurate with his knowledge of foreign languages. No one ever heard him whistle, hum a tune, or sing in worship. Other people may sing while showering; Nau never showered or sang. He used a bath tub, bucket, or tub, and talked to himself. Clemonce Sabourin was once urged by Nau to offer his critique of a mission film that had been shown in St. Louis. Nau felt that the ending of the film did not harmonize with the subject of the picture. On preview, Clemonce was surprised to discover that the inappropriate and raucous gospel song was the Hallelujah Chorus of Handel's *Messiah*.

Nau served Immanuel for 25 years. That meant he had presided over several generations of students. To the students of his early years he was both a disciplinarian and a humanitarian. He deplored laziness and encouraged honest mental and physical toil. He was thought to be fair in his dealings and enthusiastic about the entire program of the school, including athletic competition. He rooted for Immanuel, the glorious *Red and White*. A man of contradictory moods, he could crush a student against the wall and later liven up a party for students by pouring a gallon of his blackberry wine into the punch without worrying about what others might think. He found it difficult to turn away students who needed help. Often he dipped into his own pocket.

After his departure from Immanuel in 1951, students knew him only by reputation. Nevertheless, his spirit continued to influence students even after the school was closed by the church in June, 1961.

In a way, Nau gave the strong impression that he never grew up, but was always growing. And in growing the real man appeared again and again in different shades of light. In 1928 he had the opportunity to join the faculty of the University of North Carolina as a professor of languages. The salary offered was four times the amount he was receiving as president of Immanuel. He declined. Years later his sons asked him, "Why have you remained with the Lutheran Church-Missouri Synod, knowing at all times that you were not regarded a team man and therefore would never gain a position of influence and trust?"

"I am a Missouri Synod Lutheran," their father replied, "not for the purpose of furthering my own abilities, but through many years of study I have been convinced that I am closer to the Truth by being a member of such a body." Holding a silver dollar in his hand, but ignorant of what the future would do to the validity of his illustration, he pointed to the coin and said, "This is the most solid piece of money in the world. The Missouri Synod is as solid in its teachings as this silver dollar." However, when Walter joined the United Lutheran Church of America, now the Lutheran Church of America, during the 1930's, Henry wished him God's blessing and assured him that he was serving and working with Christian people and good Lutherans.

In New Orleans at a conference of ministers he suggested that it might be well for "Missouri" to institute the practice of changing pastors periodically, as was done among Methodist Christians. Life-long calls, he felt, were not based on Sacred scripture, but contributed much to spiritual laziness on the part of both the pastor and the congregation.

During his stay in Africa, Nau had encouraged leaders of the Ibibio people to give up all their wives but one. With the passage of time, he began to relax his earlier views about polygamy. He did not hold to the idea that polygamous marriages necessarily led to jealousy and strife. He dared to suggest that should a condition exist where women outnumbered men in such proportions that many women would not experience the security of marriage, a Christian man could marry more than one woman for the happiness of all.

If there was one statement which gave an insight into Nau's mind set, it was the one he made to William Kampschmidt before leaving for India in 1951. Kampschmidt asked, "Why do you want to go to India in your old age?" Henry answered, "I don't know, but I must go."

Nau left little of this world's goods. A simple, modest home, not paid for, had been his last earthly shelter in Greensboro. A small insurance policy paid the funeral expenses and left Helen a few dollars. No visible monument was erected in his honor. He would have wanted it that way. Instead, the Nau Memorial Lectures were established at the seminary in Nagercoil, India. But the memory of Nau did not depend even on this memorial, for the flow into the fund was insufficient to hold them regularly. The living joy he brought to others remained the clearest testimony to Nau's greatness.

The legacy he left was best expressed by his friend Leslie Frerking, of Charlotte, North Carolina: "Three men influenced my life the most; and one of these was Henry Nau." When Nau met someone with only a modicum of feeling for people who lacked acquaintance with Christianity, he could inspire such a person to engage in praying, giving, or going, or all three.

No one in the Lutheran Church-Missouri Synod emphasized more than did Nau the importance of liberating mission stations from dependence on the sending churches. He abhorred the spirit of colonialism that stunted Christian development in the younger churches. Inspired of God he sought to bring inspiration to others for broader vision and more extensive outreach. He did not live long enough to see his black brothers and sisters of the Lutheran Church brought into full membership. He contributed much, however, to the realization of that dream.

Someone rendered this tribute: "Men in mission do not die; their spirits live on to encourage many who follow to carry the banner of the cross gallantly, bravely, and venturesomely." Snatched like a brand from the fire, Nau lived mission inspired.

Only after Henry's death did Helen hear how her husband had spent his early years, but she refused to believe it even from the lips of one of her own sons. She outlived Henry by 15 years and enjoyed nothing so much as a good meal at a cafeteria.

Never bed-ridden, on April 13, 1971, she walked to the car that took her to a hospital in Panama City for treatment of what appeared to be a minor ailment. Five hours later she joined her husband in eternity. Her body rests next to his in Forest Lawn Cemetery at the Guilford County Courthouse Battlefield, North Carolina.

BIBLIOGRAPHY

BOOKS

Krebs, Ervin E. *The Lutheran Church and The American Negro*. Board of American Missions, American Lutheran Church, Columbus, Ohio, 1950.

Lankenau, F.J. *The World Is Our Field*. Concordia Publishing House, St. Louis, Missouri, 1928.

Mueller, John Theodore. *Brightest Light for Darkest Africa*. Concordia Publishing House, St. Louis, Missouri, 1936.

Nau, Henry. *Banji Bhumi*. Concordia Publishing House, St. Louis, Missouri, 1913.

Nau, Henry. *We Move Into Africa*. Concordia Publishing House, St. Louis, Missouri, 1945.

Nau, Henry. *Zum 25-sten, Jubilaeum — unserer Mission unter dem Tamulenvolke Osteindiens*. Johannes Herrmann, Zwickau, Saxony, U.D.

Polack, W.G. *Into All The World*. Concordia Publishing House, St. Louis, Missouri, 1930.

Volz, Paul M. *The Evangelical Lutheran Church of Nigeria, 1936-1961*. Hope Waddell Press, Calabar, Nigeria, 1961.

Zorn, Herbert, M. *Much Cause for Joy and Some for Learning*. Missouri Evangelical Lutheran India Mission, Malappuram, Kerada, 1970.

THESES

Fergin, James Arthur. "History of the India Mission of the Lutheran Church-Missouri Synod, 1945-1957." Unpublished thesis for the Bachelor of Divinity degree. Concordia Seminary, June, 1958.

Griesse, Elmer Edward. "Lutheran India Missions." Unpublished S.T.M. dissertation. Concordia Seminary, January 20, 1945.

Siler, Callie Clover. "The History of Immanuel Lutheran College, Greensboro, North Carolina, From 1903-1952." Unpublished thesis, Durham, North Carolina, 1954.

Zorn, Herbert Manthey. "The Background and the First Twenty-five Years of the Missouri Evangelical Lutheran India Mission, 1894-1919." Unpublished thesis for the Master of Sacred Theology. Concordia Seminary, June, 1969.

MAGAZINE ARTICLES

The Minaret, Volume 1, Number 1.

The Minaret, Volume 17, Number 2.

The Minaret, Volume 18, Number 1.

NEWSPAPER ARTICLES

Nau, John F. "Life in the Southern Nigeria Bush Land." *Greensboro Daily News,* March, 1937.

"Dr. and Mrs. Nau Called Upon to Give All Sorts of Advice." *Greensboro Daily News,* Greensboro, North Carolina, April 4, 1937.

"Nigerian Life Pictured by Dr. Nau." *Greensboro Daily News,* Greensboro, North Carolina, April 4, 1937.

BULLETINS

Immanuel Lutheran College, Greensboro, North Carolina, 1927-28.

Immanuel Lutheran College, Greensboro, North Carolina, 1929-30.

Immanuel Lutheran College, Greensboro, North Carolina, 1930-31.

Immanuel Lutheran College, Greensboro, North Carolina, 1935-36.

Immanuel Lutheran College, Greensboro, North Carolina, 1951-52.

Immanuel Lutheran College, Greensboro, North Carolina, 1952-53.

Immanuel Lutheran College, Greensboro, North Carolina, 1953-54.

CATALOGS

Immanuel Lutheran College, 1925.

Immanuel Lutheran College, 1926-27.

Immanuel Lutheran College, 1928-29.

Immanuel Lutheran College, 1940-41.

Immanuel Lutheran College, 1941-42.

Immanuel Lutheran College, 1946-47.

Immanuel Lutheran College, 1947-48.

ANNOUNCEMENTS

Immanuel Lutheran College, 1940-41.

Immanuel Lutheran College, 1943-44.

Immanuel Lutheran College, 1944-45.

Immanuel Lutheran College, 1945-46.

Immanuel Lutheran College, 1946-47.

Immanuel Lutheran College, 1947-48.

PRINTED REPORTS

"Twenty-seventh Report of the Board for Colored Missions," July, 1932-June, 1934.

Conference of Muslim Mission Workers, Bangalore, India, 1964, Unpublished.

LETTERS

From P. Hylant. Berlin, January 16, 1921.

From Helen Nau to John Nau. Vaniyambadi, India, January 5, 1954.

From A.O. Fuerbringer to Henry Nau. St. Louis, Missouri, March 3, 1954.

From Albert Dominick to John F. Nau. November 11, 1963.

From Clemonce Sabourin to John Nau. January 21, 1964.

From Henry J. Otten to John F. Nau. Columbus, Ohio, May 6, 1964.

From Ernest Hahn to John F. Nau. January 15, 1965.

From Clemonce Sabourin to John Nau. New York City, New York, November, 1969.

From Herbert M. Zorn to John F. Nau. Nagercoil, India, September 21, 1970.

From Ernest Hahn to John Nau. Vaniyambadi, India, March 29, 1971.

From Ernest Hahn to John Nau. Calicut, India, July, 1971.

INTERVIEWS

Dominick, Albert. Personal Interviews. Mobile, Alabama, and at various conferences and meetings, 1958, 1960, 1962, 1964.

Former students of Henry Nau. Washington, D.C., August, 1970.

Frerking, Leslie. Personal Interviews. Charlotte, North Carolina, August, 1962.

Hartmann, Christina. Personal Interview. Walluf am Rhein, Germany, September 3-4, 1965.

Hartmann, Elizabeth. Personal Interview with Henry's sister. Wiesbaden, Germany, September 7, 1965.

Kampschmidt, William. Personal Interview. Greensboro, North Carolina, August, 1962.

Nau, Conrad. Personal Interview. Norlina, North Carolina, 1960, 1961, 1964.

Nau, Eric. Personal Interview. Greensboro, North Carolina, August, 1962, 1968, 1971, 1973.

Nau, Henry (Mrs.). Personal Interview. Greensboro, North Carolina, and Panama City, Florida, 1952-1968.

Nau, J. Henry. Personal Interview. Shawano, Wisconsin, December, 1971, 1973.

Nau, Walter. Personal Interview. Hickory, North Carolina, August, 1962.

Schiebel, Walter. Personal Interview. Washington, D.C., August, 1970.

Zucker, Fredrick, Sr., and Mrs. Personal Interviews. Biloxi, Mississippi, 1969, 1970.

UNPRINTED REPORTS

Registration certificate for attendance of lectures at the University of Halle-Leipzig of May 3, 1918.

Registration certificate for attendance lectures at the University of Halle-Leipzig of September 25, 1918.

Registration certificate for attendance of lectures at the University of Halle-Leipzig of February 4, 1919.

Diploma of Vocation, Board for Colored Missions, Evangelical Lutheran Conference of North America to Henry Nau to be president of Immanuel Lutheran College at Greensboro, signed by Theodore Graebner, Chairman; C.F. Drewes, Director. (Undated)

Diploma of Doctor of Philosophy issued October, 1920, from the University of Halle-Leipzig, Germany, to Henry Nau, born in Beltershausen, a student of theology.

Baptismal certificate of Henry Nau in possession of John Nau, Hattiesburg, Mississippi.

Devotional booklet written by H. Nau, 1945, entitled "In alle Welt."

†††††

All correspondence between Nau and the Board of Missions of the Synodical Conference and of the Foreign Mission Board of the Lutheran Church-Missouri Synod in the Nau collection stored in the Concordia Historical Archives in St. Louis, Missouri.

Minutes of board meetings of the Board for Missions of the Synodical Conference and of the Foreign Mission Board of the Missouri Synod stored in the Concordia Historical Archives, St. Louis, Missouri.

Printed reports of the proceedings of the Synodical Conference from 1925-1950 stored in the Concordia Historical Archives, St. Louis, Missouri.